**Exhibition of
Chinese History**

D0128740

Editorial Direction: Yu Weichao, Du Yaoxi

Text Writers: (in order of contents)

    Li Ji, An Jiayuan, Sun Qigang, Dong Qi, Wang Guanying,
    Chen Chengjun, Wang Yonghong, Shao Xiaomeng,
    Shao Wenliang, Kong Xiangxing, Hu Xiaojian, Zheng Enhuai,
    Huang Yansheng, Chen Yu, Liu Ruzhong, Li Zefeng,
    Wang Fang, Li Xuemei, Su Shengwen

Translators: Gong Lizeng, Yang Aiwen

Photographers: Yan Zhongyi, Sun Kerang

Assistant Photographers: Shao Yulan, Liu Li, Dong Qing

Maps by: Zhang Guanying, Zhang Jie, Duan Yong, Huang Yucheng

Managing Editor: Jiang Cheng'an

Designer: Zheng Hong

Exhibition of Chinese History

Compiled by:

National Museum of Chinese History

Published by:

Morning Glory Publishers

35 Chegongzhuang Xilu Beijing 100044 China

Distributed by:

China International Book Trading Corporation

35 Chegongzhuang Xilu Beijing 100044 China

(P.O. Box 399, Beijing, China)

First Edition 1998 Second Printing 2002

ISBN 7-5054-0559-4/J.0282

85-E-515P 09750

Printed in the People's Republic of China

National Museum of Chinese History

Exhibition of Chinese History

Contents

Exhibition of Chinese History *(Level Plan and Order of Exhibits)*   5

Location of the National Museum of Chinese History   6

Preface   7

Palaeolithic Age   8-11

Evolution and Geographic Distribution of Man in
Remote Antiquity   8

Life of *Homo Erectus*   9

Life of *Homo Sapiens*   10

Neolithic Age   12-29

Advent of Agriculture   12

Primitive Clan Communities   16

Clan Tribes in Various Areas   20

Improved Farming Technology and Advent of Handicrafts   24

The Rise of Classes   26

Xia, Shang, Western Zhou, Spring and Autumn   30-59

Establishment of the Xia Dynasty and Its Culture   30

Shang Dynasty, Its Establishment and Importance   33

Economy and Culture of the Shang Dynasty   35

Establishment of the Western Zhou Dynasty   42

Ritual System and Criminal Penalties of the Western
Zhou Dynasty   45

Economy of the Western Zhou Dynasty   48

Decline of the Zhou Royal Family and
Struggles between Big Powers   50

The Economy and Culture of the Spring and Autumn Period   55

Ethnic Minorities in Peripheral Areas from the Xia Dynasty to the
Spring and Autumn Period   57

Warring States Period   60-73

Coexistence of Seven Powers   60

Economy of the Warring States Period   65

Science, Culture and Contention of a Hundred Schools   72

Peripheral Ethnics During the Warring States Period   73

Qin, Western Han and Eastern Han   74-91

Qin Unifies China   74

The Powerful and Prosperous Western Han   77

Expansion of Despotic Forces in the Eastern Han   82

Peripheral Minority Nationalities of the Han Dynasty   85

Science and Culture of the Han Dynasty   88

The Silk Road; Economic and Cultural Exchanges with Foreign
Countries in the Han Dynasty   91

**Three Kingdoms, Western and Eastern Jin, Northern and
Southern Dynasties   92-109**

Confrontation between Wei, Shu and Wu   92

Short Period of Unification under the Western Jin   95

Further Development in the South   96

Amalgamation of Nationalities in the North   98

Cultural Exchange with Foreign Countries   104

Science and Technology, Art and Culture   106

Sui, Tang and Five Dynasties   110-131

Sui Unifies the North and South   110

The Prime Tang   113

Ethnic Tribes on the Borders of the Tang Empire   116

Economy of the Tang Dynasty   117

Economic and Cultural Relations with Foreign Countries   122

Science, Culture and Social Life of the Tang Dynasty   126

Peasant Uprising in the Late Tang Dynasty and the Period of the
Five Dynasties and Ten Kingdoms   130

Song, Liao, Western Xia, Jin and Yuan   132-155

Simultaneous Existence of the Song, Liao, Western Xia and Jin   132

Economy of the Song Dynasty   140

Science and Culture of the Song Dynasty   145

Yuan Dynasty, Period of Great Unity   149

Ming Dynasty   156-167

Establishment of the Ming Dynasty   156

Economy and Social Life   158

Culture, Science and Technology   162

Foreign Relations   164

Decline of the Ming Dynasty   166

Qing Dynasty   168-187

Establishment of the Qing Dynasty   168

Economy and Social Life   172

Culture, Science and Technology   177

Economic and Cultural Exchanges with Foreign Countries
in the Early Qing   180

Decline of the Qing Dynasty   181

Economy and Culture of the Late Qing   184

End of the Last Imperial Dynasty and
Establishment of a Republic   186

Chronological Table of the Exhibition of Chinese History   188

National Museum of Chinese History; One of the Halls of the
Exhibition of Chinese History   189

Postscript   190

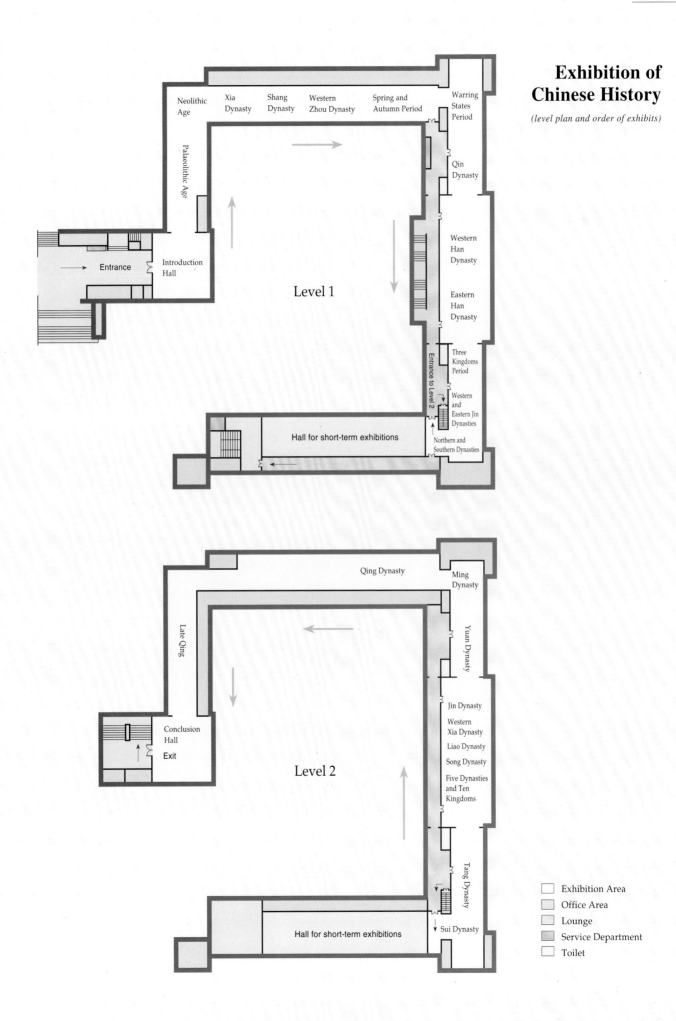

**Exhibition of
Chinese History**

(level plan and order of exhibits)

Neolithic Age

Xia Dynasty

Shang Dynasty

Western Zhou Dynasty

Spring and Autumn Period

Warring States Period

Qin Dynasty

Palaeolithic Age

Western Han Dynasty

Eastern Han Dynasty

Level 1

Entrance

Introduction Hall

Three Kingdoms Period

Entrance to Level 2

Western and Eastern Jin Dynasties

Hall for short-term exhibitions

Northern and Southern Dynasties

Qing Dynasty

Ming Dynasty

Late Qing

Yuan Dynasty

Jin Dynasty

Western Xia Dynasty

Liao Dynasty

Song Dynasty

Five Dynasties and Ten Kingdoms

Conclusion Hall

Exit

Level 2

Tang Dynasty

Hall for short-term exhibitions

Sui Dynasty

☐ Exhibition Area

☐ Office Area

☐ Lounge

☐ Service Department

☐ Toilet

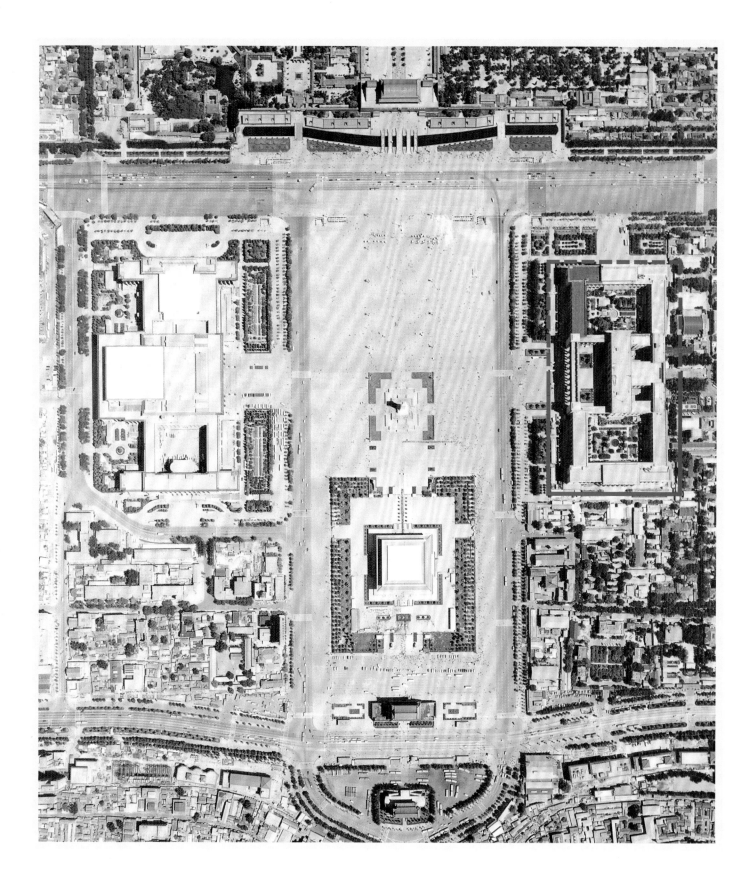

Location of the National Museum of Chinese History

Preface

China's ancient civilization is one of the few in the world with independent origins, and the only ancient civilization that has continued down to the present. Only fragments of this glorious civilization have survived, and the National Museum of Chinese History has managed to preserve some of its finest pieces — all of them relics with special scientific, historic and artistic value. Thanks to the efforts of modern scholars, they have been restored to their original place in history, and their inner connections and laws can be discerned. Now these objects not only retain their original material attributes but are endowed with the life and qualities of the artisans who made them. Through these objects, visitors to the museum and readers of this book can trace the path of history, piece together the contours of ancient citadels of civilization, witness many a soul-stirring historic event, meet the heroes and heroines of long ago, and feel the pulse of a nation traveling a rugged historic path.

History as people generally know it is built upon written words and symbols, which in an abstract manner join together people and events. What we see in the National Museum's exhibition halls, however, is history concrete and material. The clothing, ornaments and household articles on display were commonplace in their time. But the fact that they have survived the vicissitudes of several thousand years have transformed them into solid, three-dimensional expressions of history. They have given history color and substance, so that it can be seen and enjoyed. They have shortened the distance, unraveled the abstruseness and explained the mystery that separates the past from the present. They have made history more interesting, attractive and endearing. Visitors linger in the exhibition halls, staying to delve into the secrets of a remote past.

The final part of the Exhibition of Chinese History is set in 1911, when the last Chinese feudal dynasty ended and old China, braving hazards, entered a new epoch. That preparations began in the following year, 1912, for the National Museum of History, predecessor of today's museum, was not a simple coincidence. Only when a nation sets out in earnest to build a modern civilization can it fully understand how to value and appreciate its past. Today any visitor to the museum, stepping out of the silent exhibition halls on to the platform before the main entrance, and seeing the magnificent square basking in the sunshine and bustling with life, cannot but be inspired with new hope, new faith and new ideas.

Palaeolithic Age   (c.1.7 million—10,000 Years B.P.)

Archaeologists refer to the period from the rise of the human race to the eve of the appearance of agriculture as the Palaeolithic Age, which covered 99.9% of the whole course of human history and prehistory. During this period man underwent the physical evolution from *Homo erectus* to *Homo sapiens* to *Homo sapiens sapiens*; his physique evolved from that of the ape-man to that of modern man; and his cranial capacity enlarged continuously. Stone tools were the hallmark of the entire Palaeolithic Age. As time passed, simple, crude tools gave way to a growing variety of refined ones with regular shapes. The changes picked up speed and by the late Palaeolithic humans had learnt how to make and trim bone as well as stone tools and to drill holes in them. From the use and control of fire by *Homo erectus* to the discovery of ways of making fire by *Homo sapiens sapiens* was another important stage in human history. During the Upper Palaeolithic the conceptual thought of *Homo sapiens* developed rapidly and both religion and art appeared.

Evolution and Geographic Distribution of Man in Remote Antiquity

The evolution from *Homo erectus* to *Homo sapiens* to *Homo sapiens sapiens* in China was a continuous process. Yuanmou man who lived 1.7 million years ago was the earliest *Homo erectus* discovered in China. Lantian man, Peking man and Hexian man were other important members of the species but were of a slightly later date. Dali man, Maba man, Upper Cave man and Liujiang man belonged to the species *Homo sapiens*. These discoveries show that China was an important place in the evolution of man.

1-1-1

1-1-2

1-1-1 Peking Man carrying a deer (reconstruction of a sculpture)

1-1-2 Fossilized skull of Jinniushan man (replica)
Lower Palaeolithic, 12.3 cm high; unearthed in 1984 at Jinniushan, Yingkou City, Liaoning.

Life of *Homo Erectus*

Homo erectus belonged to the Lower Palaeolithic Age. Discoveries at Zhoukoudian cave near Beijing epitomize human life during this period. Among the findings were the fossils of some forty individuals, tens of thousands of stone tools, vestiges of the use of fire and the remains of food gathered or hunted.

Human labor began with the making of tools. Stone tools and wooden sticks fashioned with them, however crude and simple, could accomplish what bare fists could not. It was with these primitive tools that man gradually transformed nature and himself.

The use of fire represented a big step forward in human history. Peking man knew how to use and control fire. He used it to cook, illuminate, warm himself and keep wild beasts away. The use of fire quickened the development of his body and brain and enhanced his ability to survive harsh living conditions.

From the remains of Peking man, archaeologists have discovered not only the seeds of edible Chinese hackberries but also a large quantity of fossils of birds and animals, including those of more than 2,000 thick-jawed deer.

These discoveries show that gathering and hunting for food were Peking man's way of life.

1-2-1

1-2-1 Stone hammers and anvil Lower Palaeolithic; unearthed at Site One of Zhoukoudian, Fangshan District, Beijing.

1-2-2 Charred bone (left) and cinders Lower Palaeolithic; unearthed at Site One of Zhoukoudian, Fangshan District, Beijing. In a cave where Peking Man once lived were four layers of cinders, the thickest nearly six meters. The cinders often lay in leaps, and scattered among them were the burnt seeds of the Chinese hackberry and large quantities of charred animal bones, evidence that Peking man had learnt how to use fire.

1-2-2

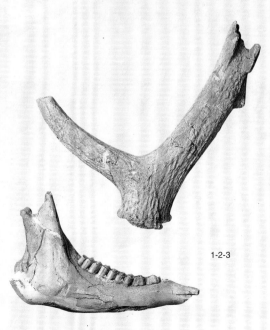

1-2-3

1-2-3 Antler and lower jawbone of thick-jawed deer Lower Palaeolithic; unearthed at Site One of Zhoukoudian, Fangshan District, Beijing.

Life of *Homo Sapiens*

By the Middle and Upper Palaeolithic, man had evolved into *Homo sapiens*. Widespread use of darts and slings, improvements made in spears and harpoons, invention of the bow and arrow, and discovery of ways to make fire — these greatly facilitated economic development in a society where hunting and fishing were the main occupations, and substantially improved man's material life. Soul worship and aesthetic concepts appeared during the Upper Palaeolithic.

The techniques of making stone tools improved somewhat during the mid-Palaeolithic and tools were more standardized in form. But it was during the Upper Palaeolithic that major breakthroughs were made in toolmaking techniques. Humans began making finely crafted stone objects; they learnt how to trim and drill holes in them; and they began using horn and bone as well as stone to make productive implements and articles of daily life. Besides bone awls, needles, spatulas and scrapers, two significant inventions of this period were the bone harpoon with detachable barbed head and the bow and arrow. The head and shaft of the harpoon were tied to each other with a piece of rope. When the harpoon was thrust into the body of a fish, the latter's struggles would detach the head from the shaft. However, the harder it struggled, the more firmly would the head be embedded in it; and the fisherman by pulling the rope could draw the fish to the shore. The harpoon was suitable for catching large-sized fish. As for the bow and arrow, which could hit targets at a distance, it enabled the hunter to bag more and bigger game.

1-3-1

1-3-2

1-3-3

1-3-1 Triangular pointed tools Middle Palaeolithic; unearthed in 1954 at Ding Village, Xiangfen County, Shanxi Province.
1-3-2 Stone balls used in hunting Middle Palaeolithic; unearthed at Xujiayao, Yanggao County, Shanxi Province.
1-3-3 Bone needle Upper Palaeolithic, remnant length 8.2 cm; unearthed at Zhoukoudian, Fangshan District, Beijing.
1-3-4 Pierced animal teeth Upper Palaeolithic; unearthed in a hilltop cave at Zhoukoudian, Fangshan District, Beijing.

Neolithic Age (c.10,000—4,000 years B.P.)

Archaeologists regard the appearance of farming and ceramics as the beginning of the Neolithic Age, during which people began to settle down to primitive farming by the slash-and-burn method and to domesticate certain wild animals, thus securing a relatively stable supply of food. They also improved their skills in fishing and hunting, and engaged in such handicrafts as pottery-making, weaving and carpentry. During the Lower Neolithic (c.10,000-5,000 years B.P.) clans and tribes grew in size and strength and large communities appeared. Religious beliefs developed in people's minds. Painted pottery, a product of Yangshao culture, is an example of their ingenuity and creativity.

During the Upper Neolithic, China's population grew rapidly and spread to all parts of the country. Distinctive cultures were created by clans living in different regions, adding richness and color to the mosaic of Chinese culture. Plowing techniques began to appear, and farm crops increased in both output and variety. In the handicrafts, there were improvements in both division of labor and technology. People had already mastered the art of copper-smelting. Along with these developments, there was a conspicuous change in the fabric of society. The rich and poor were further polarized, religion became integrated with politics, and sizeable sacrificial altars appeared. There also appeared leaders who wielded both religious and military power and constantly engaged in wars of conquest, and who built fortified cities and castles to defend themselves from attack. By this time, some clans and tribes had entered the era of civilization.

Advent of Agriculture

About 10,000 years before the present, humans gradually gave up subsistence on hunting, fishing and gathering and turned to a more productive economy. This marked the beginning of the Neolithic revolution. The advent of agriculture and animal husbandry increased food supplies. People began to lead a settled life and to engage in various handicrafts.

China is one of the earliest countries to engage in agriculture. At least seven to eight thousand years ago, Chinese peasants had begun to grow various strains of millet in the Yellow River valley and rice in the middle and lower reaches of the Yangtze.

Through long years of hunting, humans learnt how to domesticate certain docile breeds of wild animals — pigs, dogs and chicken in the north; pigs, dogs and water buffalos in the south.

Hunting, fishing and gathering were still important means of supplementing food supplies, but the tools and techniques of hunting and fishing were greatly improved.

The need for utensils to cook food, especially farm products, promoted the development of pottery-making; and in order to improve their clothing, people gradually learnt how to spin and weave.

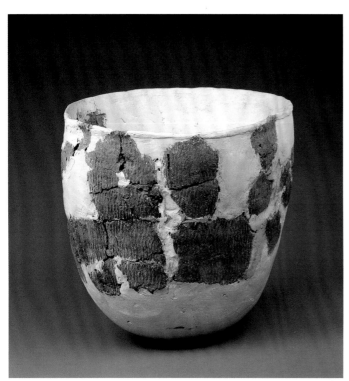

2-1-1 Clay jar Neolithic, about 10,000 years before the present, height 18 cm, mouth diameter 20 cm; unearthed in 1962 in Xianrendong (Fairy Cave), Wannian County, Jiangxi Province. It is the earliest properly shaped earthenware discovered in China to date.

2-1-2

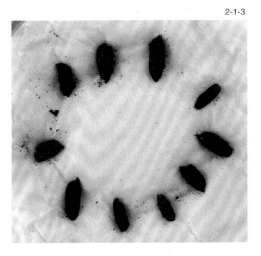

2-1-3 Rice seeds Neolithic, Hemudu culture; unearthed in 1973 at Hemudu, Yuyao County, Zhejiang Province.

2-1-4 Clay pig Neolithic, Hemudu culture, 6.7 cm long; unearthed in 1973 at Hemudu, Yuyao County, Zhejiang Province.

2-1-2 Millstone and bar Neolithic, Peiligang culture, millstone 63.5 cm long, 28 cm wide, bar 47.8 cm long; unearthed in 1978 at Peiligang, Xinzheng County, Henan Province.

2-1-4

2-1-5

2-1-6

2-1-5 Boat-shaped painted clay pot
Neolithic, Yangshao culture, 15.6 cm high,
24.8 cm wide; unearthed in 1958 at
Beishouling, Baoji, Shaanxi Province.
2-1-6 Bone spearhead for catching fish
Neolithic, 12.6 cm long; unearthed in 1985 at
Zuojiashan, Nong'an County, Jilin Province.

2-1-7 Clay bowl with cloth pattern
Neolithic, Yangshao culture, mouth
diameter of bowl 14.7 cm; unearthed in
1955 at Banpo, Xi'an, Shaanxi Province.

2-1-8 Clay spinning wheel Neolithic,
Yangshao culture, diameter 6 cm;
unearthed in 1955 at Banpo, Xi'an,
Shaanxi Province.

2-1-7

2-1-8

Primitive Clan Communities

With the development of agriculture, matriarchal clans flourished and large communities appeared. Under the matriarchal system, women played a leading role in production, genealogical systems were kept along the maternal line, and a system of exogamy was practised. The matrilineal clan was a social group pivoted on maternal blood ties; it was also a highly cohesive productive unit. Public ownership of the means of production, collective labor and the sharing of the fruits of labor among all members were the basic principles governing economic life in a matrilineal clan.

Over one hundred houses have been discovered among the ruins of a clan village with an area of 55,000 square meters in what is now Jiangzhai, Lintong, Shaanxi Province. At the center of the village is a square, surrounded by five groups of buildings. The principal building in each group is a large house, around which cluster one to two dozen small and medium-sized houses. The door of each house faces the square, symbolizing the cohesion of the matriarchal clan.

In the ruins of Jiangzhai is a tomb of a young girl. Funerary objects unearthed there include tools, clay articles and large numbers of ornaments, among which are 8,577 bone beads. The funeral objects show that women in those days were highly respected.

In a matriarchal clan society, the dead were buried in the clan's public graveyard in the order of blood relationship; when a child died, it was usually put into a jar and buried close to a house.

As production grew in scope, people's conceptual thinking was gradually enhanced and primitive forms of art and religion developed steadily. The emergence of diverse forms of sculpture and painting reflected the artistic attainment of primitive man as well as a burgeoning sense of religion in him.

2-2-1

2-2-2

2-2-1 Model of the Jiangzhai matriarchal clan village
2-2-2 Funerary objects unearthed from a young girl's tomb at Jiangzhai
2-2-3 Painted clay jar with design of stork, fish and stone axe   Neolithic, Yangshao culture, 47 cm high; unearthed in 1980 at Yan Village, Lingru County, Henan Province.

2-2-3

2-2-4 Painted pottery basin with design of fish and human face Neolithic, Yangshao culture, 16.5 cm high; unearthed in 1955 at Banpo, Xi'an, Shaanxi Province.

2-2-5 Bird-shaped ivory sculpture Neolithic, Hemudu culture, 15.8 cm long; unearthed in 1977 at Hemudu, Yuyao County, Zhejiang Province.

2-2-6 Bone flute with seven holes Neolithic, Peiligang culture, 20.4 cm long; unearthed in 1986 at Jiahu, Wuyang County, Henan Province. The flute is about 8,000 years old. It has a music scale and can be used to play simple melodies.

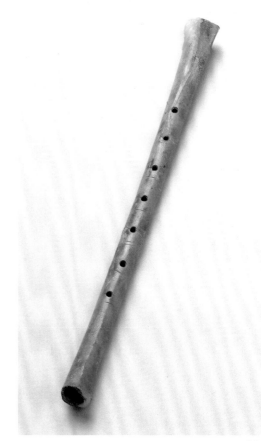

Clan Tribes in Various Areas

Primitive cultures were widely distributed on the vast territory of China. Clan tribes in various areas engaged in productive activities under different natural conditions. They created their own distinctive cultures, making great contributions to the development of ancient Chinese culture.

The chief primitive cultures are: Majiayao culture, Banshan culture and Machang culture on the upper reaches of the Yellow River; Yangshao culture and Zhongyuan Longshan culture on the middle reaches of the Yellow River; Dawenkou culture and Shandong Longshan culture on the lower reaches of the Yellow River; Daxi culture, Qujialing culture and Shijiahe culture on the middle reaches of the Yangtze; Songze culture and Liangzhu culture in the lower Yangtze valley; Fuhe culture and Hongshan culture in the northeast; Tanshishan culture and Shixia culture in the coastal areas of the south; and Karuo culture in the southwest.

2-3-1 Painted pottery jar with two ears and spiral patterns Neolithic, Majiayao culture, 50 cm high; unearthed in 1956 at Yongjing County, Gansu Province.

2-3-2 Painted pottery jar with nude bisexual figure in relief Neolithic, Machang culture, 33.4 cm high; unearthed at Liuwan, Ledu County, Qinghai Province.

2-3-1

2-3-2

2-3-2*

2-3-3

2-3-5 White pottery jug Neolithic, Dawenkou culture, 14.8 cm high; unearthed at Dawenkou, Tai'an, Shandong Province.

2-3-5

2-3-3 Terra-cotta caldron and stove Neolithic, Yangshao culture, caldron 10.9 cm high, stove 15.8 cm high; unearthed in 1956-1957 at Miaodigou, Shaan County, Henan province.

2-3-4 Gray pottery openwork stand Neolithic, Henan Longshan culture, height 33.5 cm, base diameter 35.4 cm; unearthed at Wangwan, Luoyang, Henan Province.

2-3-4

2-3-6

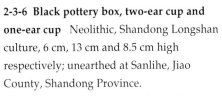

2-3-6 Black pottery box, two-ear cup and one-ear cup Neolithic, Shandong Longshan culture, 6 cm, 13 cm and 8.5 cm high respectively; unearthed at Sanlihe, Jiao County, Shandong Province.

2-3-7 Painted pottery pot with net design Neolithic, Qujialing culture, height 18.6 cm, mouth diameter 9.3 cm, base diameter 9.1 cm; unearthed in 1956 at Qujialing, Jingshan County, Hubei Province

2-3-7

2-3-8

2-3-8 Clay chicken, dog and birds Neolithic, Qujialing culture, 9.2 cm, 4 cm and 4.1 cm high respectively, unearthed at Shijiahe, Tianmen, Hubei Province.

2-3-9 Black pottery pot Neolithic, Songze culture, overall height 12.8 cm; unearthed at Guangfulin, Songjiang County, Shanghai.

2-3-9

2-3-10

2-3-11

2-3-11 Stone adze Neolithic, Tanshishan culture, 4.6 cm long, blade 3.2 cm wide; unearthed in 1964 at Tanshishan, Minhou County, Fujian Province.

2-3-12 Terra-cotta jar Neolithic, Karuo culture, 25.5 cm high; unearthed in 1978 at Karuo, Changdu County, Tibet Autonomous Region.

2-3-10 Clay tripod with flat legs Neolithic, Liangzhu culture, 31.6 cm high; unearthed in 1955 at Qianshanyang, Wuxing County, Zhejiang Province.

2-3-12

Improved Farming Technology and Advent of Handicrafts

About five thousand years ago, primitive farming technology had developed to an extent that man could obtain surplus products after meeting his basic needs. As a result, division of labor was practised more widely and handicraft workshops emerged.

This period also saw the invention of copper smelting, the potter's wheel and inlaying techniques and improvements in jade and ivory carving. Handicrafts gradually became an independent branch of production.

2-4-1 Deer-antler hoe Neolithic, 25 cm long; unearthed at Kesheng Village, Chang'an County, Shaanxi Province.
2-4-2 Stone pick-axe Neolithic, Shixia culture, 22.5 cm long, 3.7 cm wide; unearthed at Shixia, Qujiang County, Guangdong Province.

2-4-1

2-4-2

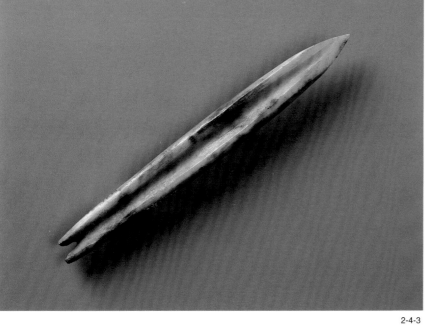

2-4-3

2-4-3 Bone shuttle Neolithic, Dawenkou culture, 16.6 cm long; unearthed at Dawenkou, Tai'an, Shandong Province.

2-4-4 Bronze knife Neolithic, Majiayao culture, 12.5 cm long; unearthed at Linjia, Dongxiang Autonomous County, Gansu Province. This knife is the earliest Chinese bronze retrieved.

2-4-5 Partitioned pottery bowl for mixing colors Neolithic, Majiayao culture, 6.5 cm high; unearthed in 1953 at Lanzhou, Gansu Province.

2-4-4

2-4-5

The Rise of Classes

The development of productivity led to the emergence of a patriarchal system and to private ownership and classes. Frequent wars of a predatory nature sped up the disintegration of the primitive society. An embryonic form of language, the appearance of ritual vessels and cities all prefigured the rise of civilization.

The advance of private ownership was predicated on the presence of surplus products and its formation was made possible by an expansion in the division of labor and the development of commodity exchange in society. Private ownership began with the possession of productive tools, articles of daily use and domestic animals. Then slaves and houses came under this system.

The advent of private ownership and classes turned what were merely revanchist conflicts between kinships into wars with property and slaves at stake. Out of the need to defend themselves and fight the enemy, tribes formed alliances and chose leaders to take control of administrative, military and religious power. Internally, these leaders protected the interests of the aristocracy and the clans they represented; externally, they waged wars for spoils. Through frequent wars some tribal leaders became hereditary aristocrats.

Towards the end of the primitive society, much headway had been made in culture, art and religion. Written language is a sa-

2-5-1

lient feature of civilization, and the origin of the Chinese written language can be traced to the patterns inscribed on Dawenkou culture earthernware. In the rise of Chinese civilization the role of shamanist priests cannot be neglected, for they not only presided over sacrificial and other ritual activities and participated in making decisions on major issues in their tribe, but also served as protectors and disseminators of science and culture, playing an important role in the beginnings of civilization.

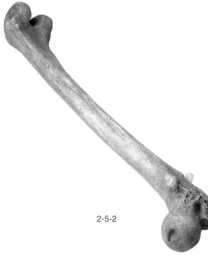

2-5-2

2-5-1 Funerary objects unearthed from Tomb No.35 at a Dawenkou graveyard
The occupants of this tomb were a couple of adults and a little girl. Many of the funerary objects unearthed from it were pottery ware and the skulls and lower jaws of pigs, which were regarded as symbols of wealth. Some tombs of the same period had only one or two funerary objects, some had none. It shows the great disparity between the rich and the poor.

2-5-3

2-5-2 Reproduction of a human leg bone with an arrow head Neolithic, Dawenkou culture; unearthed in 1963 at Dadunzi, Pei County, Jiangsu Province.

2-5-3 Clay drainpipes Neolithic, Henan Longshan culture, each section of pipe 35- 45 cm long; unearthed at Pingliangtai, Huaiyang County, Henan Province.

2-5-4 Jade pig-dragon Neolithic, Hongshan culure, 7.2 cm high; unearthed at Niuheliang, Chaoyang, Liaoning Province.

2-5-5 Jade dragon Neolithic, Hongshan culture, 26 cm high; unearthed in 1971 at Sanxingtala, Ongniud Banner, Inner Mongolia Autonomous Region.

2-5-4

2-5-5

2-5-6

**2-5-6 Painted pottery basin with figures of
dancers**   Neolithic, Majiayao culture, 14 cm
high; unearthed in 1973 at Shangsunjia Village,
Datong Hui-Tu Autonomous County, Qinghai
Province.
2-5-7 Owl-shaped *ding* (tripod)   Neolithic,
Yangshao culture, 35.8 cm high; unearthed in
1958 at Taipingzhuang, Hua County, Shaanxi
Province.

2-5-7

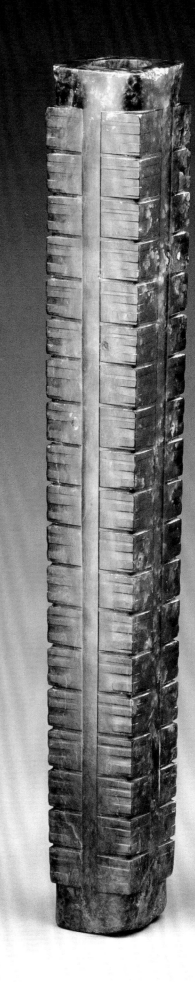

2-5-8 Jade *cong* (square column with hole in the middle) Neolithic Age, 49.7 cm high; obtained in Shandong Province.

2-5-9 Thin-shelled pottery goblet Neolithic, Shandong Longshan culture, 13 cm high; unearthed between 1974 and 1975 at Sanlihe, Jiao County, Shandong Province.

2-5-9

Xia , Shang ,Western Zhou, Spring and Autumn

(c.21st Century BC—476BC)

Establishment of the Xia Dynasty and Its Culture

Legend has it that around the 21st century BC a man called Yu (posthumously honored as Yu the Great) succeeded in taming rivers and controlling floods in China, whereby his tribe, the Xia, acquired a dominant position in the Central Plains. After his death, his son, Qi, became the tribal chief, establishing a hereditary system of rule and the first monarchic dynasty in Chinese history – the Xia Dynasty. According to historical records, the domain of Xia was located in what is now west Henan and south Shanxi provinces. The distribution and duration of Erlitou culture, which centered on the site of Erlitou in Yanshi County, Henan Province, basically coincided with the time and place of the Xia people's activities. Agriculture dominated the economic life of the people at the time, with productive tools mostly made of stone, bone and clamshell. A small number of ritual vessels, weapons and tools were made of bronze. The bronze *jue*, a tripod, was cast by the sectional piece-mold method, an indication that the making of bronzeware had already gone through a process of development. Exquisite jadeware were also made during this period, along with which there appeared a new technology of inlaying jade into bronze.

3-1-1 Portrait of Yu the Great Rubbing of a stone engraving of the Eastern Han at Wuliang Temple, Jiaxiang County, Shandong Province.

3-1-2 Reconstruction of Erlitou Palace This palace building at Erlitou was a prototype of traditional Chinese palace architecture.

3-1-3 Pottery *ding* Cooking vessel of Xia, 20.5 cm high, rim 20 cm in diameter; unearthed in 1973 at Erlitou, Yanshi County, Henan Province.

3-1-1

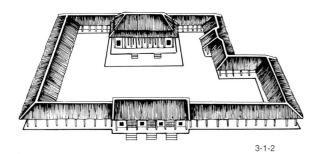

3-1-2

3-1-3

3-1-4

3-1-5

3-1-6

3-1-4 Bronze *jue* Wine goblet of Xia, 13.5 cm high, spout 14.5 cm long; unearthed in 1984 at Erlitou, Yanshi County, Henan Province. This is the earliest Chinese bronze vessel unearthed so far.

3-1-5 Pottery *he* Wine vessel of Xia, 20 cm high, belly 15.5 cm wide; unearthed in 1972-1973 at Erlitou, Yanshi County, Henan Province.

3-1-6 Stone mold Implement for bronze casting in two parts, Xia, 6.5 -7.4 cm wide, 3.4 - 3.9 cm thick, (left) 13.6 and (right) 13.8 cm long; unearthed in 1974 at Dongxiafeng, Xia County, Shanxi Province.

3-1-7 Engraved signs on pottery vessels of Erlitou culture Signs found on pottery, engraved by potters to represent certain meanings. Presumably they had something to do with the later invention of Chinese characters.

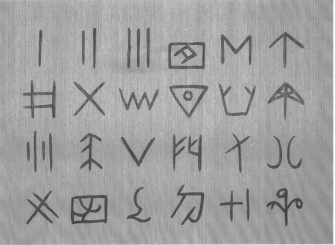

3-1-7

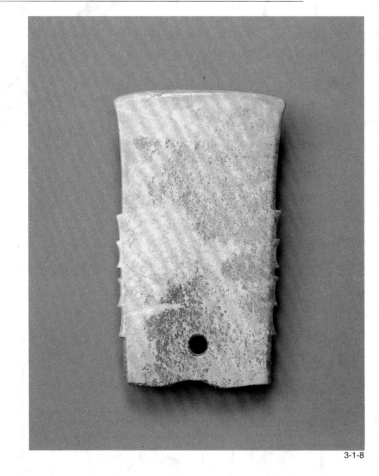

3-1-8

3-1-9

3-1-8 Jade *yue* Battle-axe of Xia, 11.3 cm long, blade 7 cm wide; unearthed in 1974 at Erlitou, Yanshi County, Henan Province. The jade *yue* was a ritual object and also a symbol of power.

3-1-9 Oracle bone Instrument for divinations, Xia Dynasty, 12 cm long; unearthed at Luoda Temple, Zhengzhou, Henan Province. This is a sheep's shoulder blade. Most of the oracle bones of the Xia Dynasty were not holed or treated in any way.

3-1-10 Stone *qing* Percussion instrument of Xia. 66.8 cm long, 28.6 cm wide; unearthed in 1974 at Dongxiafeng, Xia County, Shanxi Province. Discovery of this *qing* shows that musical instruments for ceremonies had appeared as early as the Xia Dynasty.

3-1-10

Shang Dynasty, Its Establishment and Importance

Toward the end of the Xia Dynasty, the Shang tribe that inhabited the lower reaches of the Yellow River had extended its influence to the middle reaches of the Yellow River, into areas ruled by the Xia. In the 16th century BC, the Shang leader, Tang, conquered the Xia and established the Shang Dynasty, which was to be an important stage in the development of ancient Chinese states. Large quantities of archaeological finds, especially oracle-bone inscriptions, have furnished valuable information on the history of this dynasty. In the beginning it had its capital at Bo (south of present-day Cao County, Shandong Province); eventually it moved its seat to Yin (now Anyang, Henan Province).

It maintained its rule for more than 600 years, during which it continually strengthened the state apparatus and made notable progress in the cultural and economic fields. Its social activities were more numerous and its influence on later periods far greater than those of the Xia Dynasty. Shang culture laid the foundation for a further development of ancient Chinese culture, and holds an important place in the history of the world's oldest civilizations.

3-2-1

3-2-1 Sketch map showing ruins of the Shang Dynasty in Zhengzhou   The ruins were discovered in 1952 in Zhengzhou, Henan Province. They cover an area of 25 square kilometers, in the middle of which are the remains of an early Shang city, rectanglar in shape and surrounded by a 6,960-meter-long city wall.

3-2-2 Square *ding* with nipple design   Cooking vessel, Shang Dynasty, height 100 cm, weight 82.55 kg; unearthed in 1974 in Zhengzhou, Henan Province. This *ding* is the largest of the early Shang weighty bronzes discovered so far.

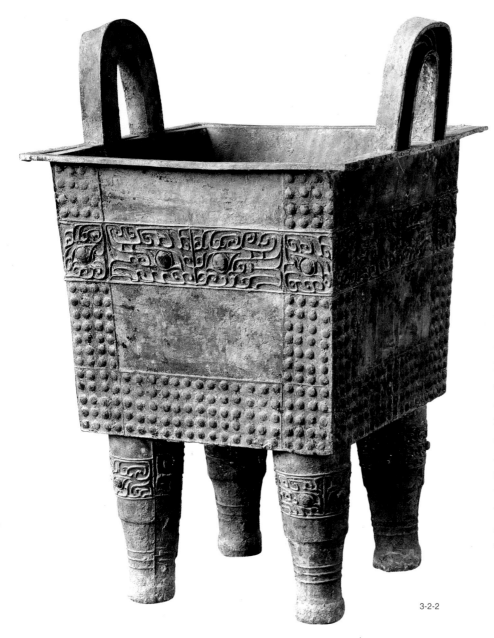

3-2-2

3-2-3 Jade *ge* (dagger-axe)   Ritual object, Shang Dynasty, overall length about 62 cm, length of blade 48.8 cm, length of tang 10.1 cm; unearthed in 1974 at Panlongcheng, Huangpi County, Hubei Province.

3-2-4 Sketch map showing the Yin ruins in Anyang   Yin, capital of the late Shang, was located in what is now northwestern Anyang, Henan Province. The ruins are dispersed over an area of about 24 square kilometers.

安阳殷墟遗址分布示意图

3-2-4

Economy and Culture of the Shang Dynasty

A brilliant bronze culture was created during the Shang Dynasty, which deserves to be called the zenith of China's Bronze Age. Bronze casting became the country's foremost handicraft industry. Diverse forms of composite-mold casting were in wide use, and numerous finely crafted and intricately shaped bronze objects were produced. Most of them were ritual vessels and weapons, but bronze tools were also used in farming, though the number was small. Agriculture was still the principal productive occupation, so much so that the term *zhongren* (literally "the masses") generally meant the peasantry in those days. Dark green glazed pottery made of kaolin dating from the Shang possessed the basic characteristics of porcelain. Some bronze vessels of the Shang had traces of silk fabrics on their surface, including plain-woven fabrics of spun silk and damask with lozenge design, suggesting that the Shang people already had an apparatus similar to the jacquard loom. Among other crafts of this period, lacquer paint-ing was widely used and practiced, and carved and engraved works were vivid in design and exquisite in workmanship. Commercial activities appeared in the early Shang, and vehicles became important means of transportation. In music, Shang musicians already had concepts of semitones and standard tones, the introduction of semitone intervals paving the way for the invention of the twelve-tone temperament. The characters in the oracle-bone inscriptions of the Shang were akin to Han characters in their basic structure, and may be regarded as a mature form of written language.

3-3-1

3-3-1 Pottery mold for casting the bronze *li*
(caldron)　Relic of the early Shang, 23 cm long, 24 cm wide; unearthed in 1954 at Nanguanwai, Zhengzhou, Henan Province.

3-3-2 Three-*yan* steamer　Cooking vessel of the late Shang, 68 cm high, 103.7 cm long; unearthed in 1976 from the Fu Hao tomb in the Yin ruins of Anyang, Henan Province. A *yan* is a vessel for steaming food.

3-3-2

3-3-4

3-3-3 Owl-shaped *zun* Bronze wine vessel of the late Shang, 45.9 cm high; unearthed in 1976 from the Fu Hao tomb in the Yin ruins of Anyang, Henan Province. This *zun* is considered a gem in Shang bronzes.

3-3-4 Bronze *yue* (battle-axe) **with iron blade** Weapon of the Shang Dynasty, 8.7 cm long; unearthed in 1977 in Pinggu County, Beijing. A laboratory test showed that the blade of this *yue* was forged from meteoric iron.

3-3-5 Bronze *yue* (battle-axe) Weapon of the Shang Dynasty, 31.7 cm long, 35.8 cm wide; unearthed in 1965 at Subutun, Yidu, Shandong Province. An inscription of two characters, *ya chou*, was cast below each of the two ears.

3-3-6 Si Mu Wu *ding* Cooking vessel of the late Shang, 133 cm high, rim 110 cm long and 79 cm wide, weight 832.84 kg; unearthed in 1939 at Wuguan Village, Anyang, Henan Province. This *ding* is the heaviest of the ancient Chinese bronzes discovered so far.

3-3-3

3-3-5

3-3-7   3-3-8

3-3-9

3-3-7 Bronze *jue* (pickaxe) Farm tool of the early Shang, 16.4 cm long, 6 cm wide; unearthed at Erligang, Zhengzhou, Henan Province. The bronze *jue* first appeared in the Shang Dynasty.

3-3-8 Bronze *chan* (shovel) Farm tool of the late Shang, 17 cm long, blade 8.8 cm wide; unearthed in 1976 from the Fu Hao tomb in the Yin ruins of Anyang, Henan Province.

3-3-9 Ox bone with inscription Shang Dynasty, 14.8 cm long, 12.5 cm wide; said to have been discovered in Anyang, Henan Province. The inscription on the bone says that a Shang king ordered peasants to farm collectively.

3-3-10 Primitive porcelain *zun* Wine container of the early Shang, 11.5 cm high, rim 18.3 cm in diameter; unearthed in 1953 in Zhengzhou, Henan Province. The oldest Chinese primitive porcelains retrieved so far date from the early Shang.

3-3-11 Jade silkworm Relic of the late Shang, 3.1 cm long; unearthed in 1953 at Dasikong Village, Anyang, Henan Province.

3-3-12 Bronze piece with remains of silk Shang Dynasty, 19.8 cm long, 14.1 cm wide; unearthed in 1953 at Dasikong Village, Anyang, Henan Province. The silk remains on this bronze piece are the earliest specimens of plain silk retrieved so far.

3-3-10

3-3-11

3-3-12

3-3-13

3-3-14

3-3-15

3-3-13 Lacquer fragments Shang Dynasty, 0.1 cm thick; unearthed in 1973 from a tomb at Taixi, Gaocheng County, Hebei Province.

3-3-14 Jade figurine Ornament of the late Shang, 7 cm high; unearthed in 1976 from the Fu Hao tomb in the Yin ruins of Anyang, Henan Province. The figurine shows the costume and headdress usually worn by people in the Shang Dynasty.

3-3-15 Bronze *wei* (axle endpiece) Parts of a carriage of the Shang Dynasty, one 15.5 cm long and 5 cm in diameter, the other 15.6 cm long and 4.8 cm in diameter; unearthed from a Shang carriage pit at Dasikong Village, Anyang, Henan Province.

3-3-16 Set of five *nao* (big cymbal) Percussion instrument of the late Shang, the biggest 14.4 cm high and the smallest 7.7 cm high; unearthed in 1976 from the

3-3-16

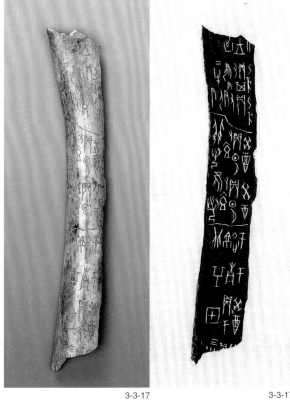

3-3-17   3-3-17*

Fu Hao tomb in the Yin ruins of Anyang, Henan Province. All five *nao* are inscribed with two characters *ya qiang* on the inside wall.

3-3-17 Oracle bone with record of solar eclipse Shang Dynasty, approximately 12 cm long; unearthed in Anyang, Henan Province. This oracle bone is valuable for studying the astronomy and calendar of the Shang Dynasty.

3-3-18 Ox bone inscribed with a table of the Heavenly Stems and Earthly Branches Shang Dynasty, 22.5 cm long and 6.6 cm wide; unearthed from the Yin ruins of Anyang, Henan Province. The calendrical system of Heavenly Stems and Earthly Branches originated in the Xia Dynasty, and was inherited by the Shang and Zhou and passed down to modern times. It is the oldest calendrical system in use in the world today.

3-3-18

3-3-18*

Establishment of the Western Zhou Dynasty

The Zhou was an ancient tribe that inhabited areas of what is now Shaanxi and Gansu provinces in northwestern China. In the 11th century BC or thereabout, King Wu of Zhou, in alliance with neighboring tribes, defeated the Shang army at Muye, overthrew the Shang Dynasty and established the Zhou, which during its early years had its capital at Feng and Hao, both near present-day Xi'an, Shaanxi Province. Historians called it the Western Zhou to distinguish it from the later Eastern Zhou that had its capital at Luoyi (now Luoyang, Henan Province) to the east. King Wu died of illness the year after he overthrew the Shang and the Duke of Zhou, one of his younger brothers, became regent. Guanshu and Caishu, two other brothers of King Wu, in league with scions of the Shang royal family, rebelled against the Zhou. After putting down the rebellion, the duke moved some adherents of the defunct Shang Dynasty to Luoyi, where he built an Eastern Capital called Chengzhou. At the same time, he enfeoffed large numbers of feudal lords in the hope that the vassal states thus created could be buffers to protect the Zhou court.

3-4-1

3-4-1 Oracle bone with numerical inscriptions Western Zhou, 13 cm long; unearthed in Chang'an County, Shaanxi Province.

3-4-2 Li *gui* Food container of Western Zhou, 28 cm high; unearthed in Lintong County, Shaanxi Province. Carved on the inside of the bottom of this *gui* is an inscription of 32 characters, recording King Wu of Zhou's defeat of the Shang army on the morning of *jiazi* day.

3-4-2*

3-4-2

3-4-3

3-4-3*

3-4-3 Tianwang *gui* Food container of Western Zhou, 24.2 cm high; said to have been unearthed in Qishan County, Shaanxi Province. On the inside bottom of this *gui* is an inscription of 78 characters, recording that after conquering the Shang, King Wu held a grand ceremony in "Heaven's Hall" at which he made offerings to his deceased father King Wen and presided over sacrifices to deities in Heaven.

3-4-4 Yi Hou Ze *gui* Food container of Western Zhou, 15.7 cm high; unearthed at Dantu County, Jiangsu Province. On the inside bottom of the *gui* is an inscription of over 120 characters, an important piece of historical material concerning the enfeoffment system of the Western Zhou Dynasty.

3-4-5 Kang Hou axe Weapon of Western Zhou, 9.1 cm long, blade 6.8 cm wide, handle 3.7 cm wide; said to have been unearthed in Jun County, Henan Province. Inscribed on it are the two characters for "Kang Hou" (Marquis Kang), a younger brother of King Wu.

3-4-4*

3-4-5*

3-4-5

3-4-4

3-4-6**

3-4-6 Yan Hou *yu* Food container of
Western Zhou, 24 cm high; unearthed in
the Mongolia Autonomous County of
Harqin Left Wing, Liaoning Province.
Inscribed on the inside wall of the *yu* are
five characters showing that it was made
on the order of the Marquis of Yan. Yan
was a vassal state enfeoffed in the early
Zhou Dynasty.

3-4-6*

3-4-6

Ritual System and Criminal Penalties of the Western Zhou Dynasty

The Western Zhou that succeeded the Shang was another flourishing period of the Bronze Age in China. Basing themselves on blood relations, Western Zhou rulers established a comprehensive patriarchal, hierarchic and hereditary enfeoffment system, and a strict system of rites and criminal penalties. Zhou rites were based on the patriarch clan system and contained a host of rules and regulations to give expression to hierarchical differences, the purpose being to regulate relations within the ruling class. Different ritual vessels and different ways of grouping them were instituted for noblemen at different levels. Commoners were not allowed to use rituals reserved only for the nobility. Various criminal penalties were used as a means to keep commoners and slaves under control.

3-5-1 Chang Xin *bian zhong* (chime of bells) Percussion instrument of Western Zhou, height 38.5-48 cm, distance between rim angles 25.4 - 27.5 cm; unearthed at Pudu Village, Chang'an County, Shaanxi Province. *Bian zhong* was the main ritual instrument played at sacrificial activities or feasts of aristocrats in the Western Zhou Dynasty.

3-5-2 Lid of Guo Cong *gui* Lid of a food container, Western Zhou, height 7 cm, rim diameter 24.6 cm. On the inside of the lid is an inscription of 96 characters. It contains a fairly complete record of a lawsuit concerning a farmland dispute, and is of reference value to the study of the land system and legal proceedings of the Western Zhou Dynasty.

3-5-2

3-5-2*

3-5-1

3-5-3*

3-5-3

3-5-3 Da Yu *ding*   Cooking vessel, Western Zhou, height 101.9 cm, mouth diameter 77.8 cm; said to have been unearthed in Mei County, Shaanxi Province. On the inside wall of the *ding* is an inscription of 291 characters in 19 lines, which says that King Kang of Zhou enfeoffed an aristocrat Yu in the ninth month of the 23rd year of his reign.

3-5-4 Yu *ding*   Cooking vessel of Western Zhou, height 54.6 cm; said to have been unearthed in Qishan County, Shaanxi Province. On the inside wall of its belly is an inscription of 207 characters, recording the Zhou court's relations with South Huaiyi and East Yi, ancient tribes in southeastern China, as well as the Western Zhou's military system.

3-5-5 Guo Ji Zi Bai *pan*   Water container of Western Zhou, length 137.2 cm, width 86.5 cm, height 39.5 cm, weight 215.3 kg; unearthed in Baoji, Shaanxi Province. On the inside bottom of the *pan* is an inscription of 110 characters. It is the biggest bronze ware of the Shang-Zhou period discovered so far.

3-5-4*

3-5-4

3-5-5

Economy of the Western Zhou Dynasty

Both economy and culture continued to develop during the Western Zhou. In the latter part of this dynasty, elements of a new relationship of production began to appear, and society was on the eve of a great transformation. According to Western Zhou's land system, all land in the country nominally belonged to the king. This was expressed in the saying, "There is no land under heaven that is not the king's land." Aristocrats and commoners alike received a share of the land from the king. They had the right to use the land, but were forbidden to transfer, buy or sell it. In metallurgy, after the mid-Zhou period new techniques made it possible to cast long inscriptions on many bronze vessels. The making of primitive porcelain was more popular than before, and tiles were used on buildings for the first time in Chinese history.

3-6-1*

3-6-1 Zhao *you* Wine container of Western Zhou, height 9.5 cm. Inside the *you* is an inscription of 44 characters, recording that a Zhou king bestowed on a man named Zhao 50 square *li* of land in Bidi. It is an important piece of material for the study of the ancient well-field system of land allocation.

3-6-2 Gebo *gui* Food container, Western Zhou; height 31 cm. Inside the *gui* is an inscription of 82 characters that tells about the exchange of land during the Western Zhou period.

3-6-3 Diao Sheng *gui* Food container, Western Zhou, height 22.2 cm, mouth diameter 21.9 cm, base diameter 18 cm. Inside the *gui* is an inscription of 104 characters, recording a lawsuit in which Diao Sheng, with the help of the chief of his clan, received more land than his rightful share.

3-6-1

3-6-2*

3-6-3*

3-6-2

3-6-3

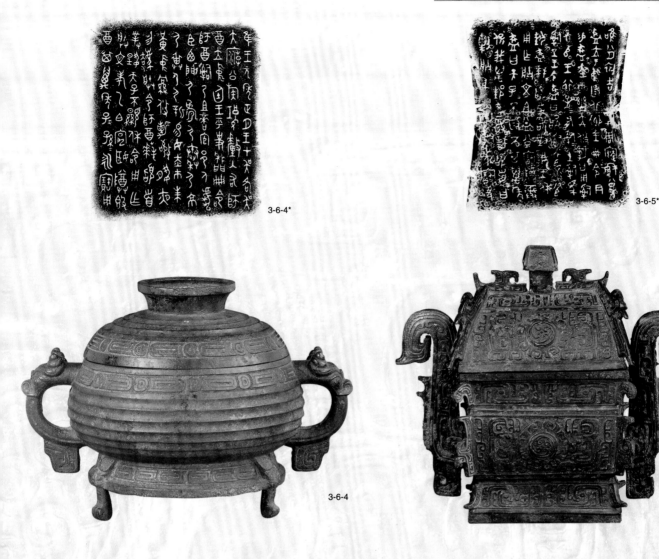

3-6-4*

3-6-5*

3-6-4

3-6-5

3-6-4 Shi You *gui* Food container, Western Zhou, total height 22.5 cm, rim diameter 19.1 cm, base diameter 20 cm. On the inside wall of both the body and the cover of the *gui* is an inscription of 106 characters, recording that King Yi of Zhou ordered Shi You to succeed to the post of his ancestors who were overseers of farm workers and slaves.

3-6-5 Li fang *yi* Wine container, Western Zhou, height 22.8 cm; unearthed in Mei County, Shaanxi Province. A long inscription on its inside wall tells about the military system of the Western Zhou Dynasty.

3-6-6 Plain tiles Western Zhou, width 24 cm; unearthed in Fufeng County, Shaanxi Province. In China, tiles were first used on buildings during the early years of the Western Zhou.

3-6-6

Decline of the Zhou Royal Family and Struggles between Big Powers

In 770 BC King Ping of Zhou moved his capital to Luoyi (present-day Luoyang, Henan Province). This marked the beginning of what is called the Spring and Autumn Period in Chinese history, a period of great upheavals. After the removal of its seat to the east, the power and prestige of the Zhou royal family declined, and feudal lords began fighting each other for supremacy. Duke Huan of Qi, Duke Wen of Jin, Prince Zhuang of Chu, Duke Mu of Qin and the kingdoms of Wu and Yue successively gained hegemony in the country. In the late Spring and Autumn Period, the chancellors and ministers of various fiefdoms became powerful and there appeared a situation in which "all rituals, ceremonies and expeditions are masterminded by high officials."

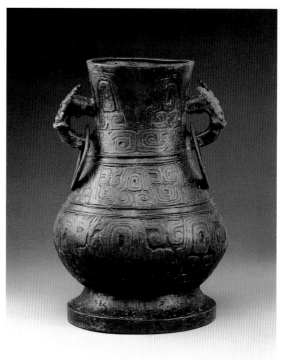

3-7-1

3-7-2

Province. The *bo* bears an inscription of 173 characters. It records that because of what Bao Shu, Ming's grandfather, did for the state of Qi, the marquis of Qi granted Ming lordship over several manor estates and the people living on them. Ming regarded this as an encouragement and cast the *bo* as a sacrificial vessel to his deceased mother Zhong Jiang.

3-7-3

3-7-1 Huan Zi's Meng Jiang *hu* Wine or water container, Spring and Autumn Period, height 22.1 cm, mouth diameter 13.4 cm. On the inside wall of the neck of this *hu* is an inscription of 142 characters, recording that after the death of Huan Zi's father, the marquis of Qi asked and obtained permission from the king of Zhou to hold various ceremonies for the deceased.

3-7-2 Ming *bo* Musical instrument, Spring and Autumn Period, height 66 cm, mouth length 44 cm, mouth width 34.8 cm; unearthed in 1870 at Houtuci, Ronghe County, Shanxi

3-7-4

3-7-3 Bronze *hu* inlaid with copper bird-and-beast designs
Wine or water container, Spring and Autumn Period, height
32 cm; said to have been unearthed in 1923 at Jiyu Village,
Hunyuan County, Shanxi Province. Hunyuan was the site of
ancient Dai, a state established by a northern tribe in the late
Spring and Autumn Period, and conquered by the state of
Zhao in the early Warring States Period.

3-7-4 Bronze Square *hu* Wine or water container, Spring
and Autumn Period, height 84.5 cm; unearthed in 1961 in
Houma, Shanxi Province. During the Spring and Autumn
Period, the state of Jin in its last years had its capital at Xintian
near present-day Houma. The site was discovered in 1952.

3-7-5 Prince Wu's *ding* Cooking vessel, Spring and Autumn
Period, height 67 cm, mouth diameter 66 cm; unearthed in
1979 from Grave Two at Xiasi, Zhechuan County, Henan
Province. Prince Wu, the maker of the vessel, was a son of
Duke Zhuang of Chu, one of the powerful overlords of the
Spring and Autumn Period.

3-7-5*

3-7-3*

3-7-5

3-7-6*

3-7-6

3-7-6 Duke of Qin's *gui* Food container, Spring and Autumn Period, height 19.8 cm, rim diameter 18 cm; said to have been unearthed in 1924 in Tianshui County, Gansu Province. Inside the *gui* is an inscription of 123 characters, recording that Duke Jing of Qin continued the work of his ancestors, pledging to preserve forever the lands they had owned.

3-7-7 Prince Guang of Wu's *jian* Water container, Spring and Autumn Period, height 35 cm, mouth diameter 57 cm; unearthed in 1955 from the grave of Marquis Cai, Shou County, Anhui Province. On the inside wall of the bronze *jian* is an inscription of 52 characters, showing that it was made on the order of Prince Guang of Wu as part of his daughter's dowry.

3-7-8 Sword of Fu Chai, Prince of Wu Spring and Autumn Period, total length 59.1 cm, blade width 5 cm; unearthed in 1976 in Hui County, Henan Province. Near the *xin* (part between the blade and handle) is an inscription of 10 characters in official script, showing that it was a sword used by Fu Chai.

3-7-8

3-7-7

3-7-7*

3-7-9 Bronze bird-shaped *ding* (tripod)
Cooking vessel, Spring and Autumn
Period, height 16 cm, length 22.9 cm;
unearthed in 1952 at Jiagezhuang,
Tangshan, Hebei Province. The place
where it was unearthed belonged to Yan,
a vassal state whose rulers had the same
surname as the royal family of the Zhou
Dynasty.

3-7-9

3-7-9*

3-7-10 Marquis Shen of Cai's *fang fu*
Wine or water container, Spring and
Autumn Period, height 79.8 cm, mouth
18.5 x 18.3 cm; unearthed in 1955 from the
grave of a marquis of Cai in Shou County,
Anhui Province. On the inside wall of the
neck of the *fu* is an inscription of six
characters, showing that the container was
made on the order of Marquis Shen of Cai,
who was also called Marquis Zhao.

3-7-11 Prince Ying Ci's stove An
apparatus for burning charcoal, Spring
and Autumn Period, height 11.3 cm; said
to have been unearthed in 1923 at Lijialou,
Xinzheng County, Henan Province. On
the inside wall of the stove is an
inscription of seven characters, showing
that its owner was Prince Ying Ci, who
may have been a son of the Prince of Wu.

3-7-11*

3-7-10

3-7-11

3-7-12

3-7-12 Bo Da Fu's *gui* of the State of Lu
Food container, Spring and Autumn Period, height 25.4 cm, mouth diameter 20.1 cm; unearthed in 1970 at Beichaogou, Licheng County, Shandong Province. On the bottom of the *gui* is an inscription of 18 characters, saying that it was made on the order of Bo Da Fu of the State of Lu as dowry for a young girl surnamed Ji.

3-7-13 Dagger-axe of Yuan Tu, crown prince of Guo A weapon with a bladed head, Spring and Autumn Period, total length 17.1 cm; unearthed in 1957 from Grave 1052 in a graveyard of the State of Guo at Shangcunling, Sanmenxia, Henan Province. On the head is a 6-character inscription, recording that the axe belonged to Yuan Tu, crown prince of Guo, who evidently was the occupant of the grave.

3-7-13

3-7-14 Zhong You Fu *hu* of the State of Zeng
Wine or water container, Spring and Autumn Period, height 66 cm; unearthed in 1966 in Jingshan County, Hubei Province. On the inside of the cover of the hu and on the inside wall of its mouth is an inscription of 12 characters, showing that the vessel was made by Zhong You Fu of the State of Zeng.

3-7-14*

3-7-14

The Economy and Culture of the Spring and Autumn Period

With the wide use of ironware, productivity of the Spring and Autumn Period developed at an unprecedented speed. By this time people had not only learnt how to make use of forged iron but also mastered the advanced technology of pig iron smelting. The use of iron implement made large-scale land reclamation possible, promoted the development of privately owned land, and provided craftsmen with sharper and better tools. In bronze casting, a new technology of inlaying gold, silver and copper was invented. Excavation of large numbers of ceramic casting molds at Houma shows that bronze casting and mining were being undertaken on a sizable scale and had reached a high technological level. After the mid-Spring and Autumn Period, metal coins were widely used in some states. Their circulation helped promote the development of handicrafts and commerce. In the ideological sphere, this was a period of great social transformation. Eminent thinkers and educators like Laozi and Confucius and military strategists like Sun Wu emerged, whose theories had a profound impact on later generations.

3-8-1 Iron sword with gold pommel and crosspiece A weapon, Spring and Autumn Period, length 38.7 cm; unearthed in 1957 at Houchuan, Shaan County, Henan Province. It is one of a small number of ironwares of the Spring and Autumn Period so far discovered.
3-8-2 Bronze joint shaped like a capenter's square Spring and Autumn Period, length 42 cm, width 16 cm; unearthed between 1973 and 1974 at Yaojiagang, Fengxiang County, Shaanxi Province. Very few such joints have been discovered.

3-8-3 Luan Shu's *fou* Wine or water jar, Spring and Autumn Period; height 48.8 cm, mouth diameter 16.5 cm. This *fou* was made by the descendants of Luan Shu as a vessel used in sacrifices to their ancestors, but it has always been called Luan Shu's *fou*.

3-8-1

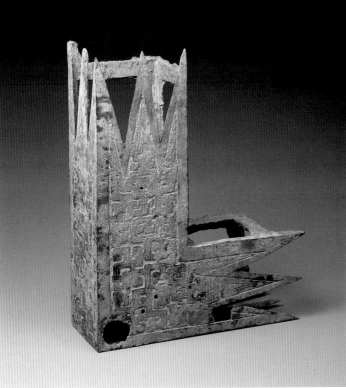

3-8-2

3-8-3

3-8-4

3-8-5

3-8-4 Pottery mold in the shape of a beast's head Spring and Autumn Period, length of remnant 8.1 cm, height 11 cm, thickness 6.2 cm; unearthed in 1961 among the ruins of a bronze foundry in Houma, Shanxi Province. The mold shows that bronze casting techniques had attained a high level by this time.

3-8-5 *Kong shou bu* coins China's earliest metal coins, Spring and Autumn Period. The coins with shrugged shoulders unearthed in 1956 in Houma, Shanxi Province, are fairly big in size, being 13 to 15 cm in height. Each coin weighs between 34 and 44 grams, including the clay core.

3-8-6 *The Art of War* copied on bamboo slips Unearthed in 1972 from Han Tomb One at Yinqueshan, Linyi County, Shandong Province. A complete slip is 27.6 cm long, written in official script. The number of characters on a slip differed, a complete slip containing on the average around 35 characters. The copies were made during the reigns of Emperors Wen and Jing and the early years of the reign of Emperor Wu of the Western Han.

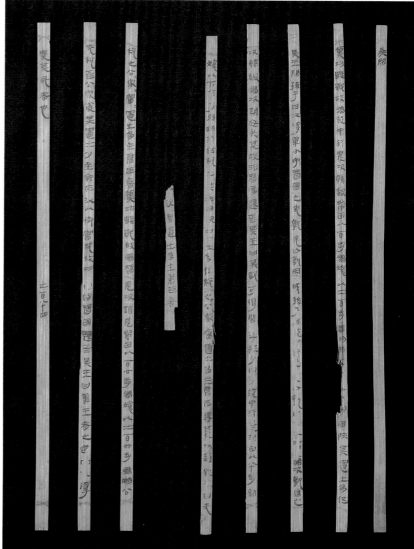

3-8-6

Ethnic Minorities in Peripheral Areas from the Xia Dynasty to the Spring and Autumn Period

The Huaxia nationality, predecessor of the Chinese nation, was formed and developed through the gradual mergence of many different nationalities. In the beginning, the term Huaxia referred mainly to the people inhabiting the Central Plains of the Yellow River valley during the Xia, Shang and Zhou dynasties. They had a highly developed economy and culture and were the first to enter class society and establish primitive states. From the Xia through the Spring and Autumn Period was a formative stage for various ethnic groups inhabiting the peripheral areas of the Central Plains. In the course of their development, their cultures with their local features and characteristics came into frequent contact with the Huaxia culture of the Central Plains, with which they gradually merged and mingled. This mergence has had a tremendous influence on the subsequent formation and development of the Han nationality and its culture.

3-9-1

3-9-1 Bronze *ding* Cooking vessel of the lower stratum of Xiajiadian culture, height 53.9 cm, mouth diameter 37.7 cm; unearthed at Ongniud Banner, Chifeng, Inner Mongolia Autonomous Region. This *ding* is a relic of the early stage of the Bronze Age in north China.

3-9-2 Bronze *zun* with dragon-tiger design Wine container of Shang period, height 50.5 cm, mouth diameter 44.9 cm; unearthed in 1957 in Funan County, Anhui Province. This *zun* belongs to Huaiyi culture. It is a rare piece among bronzeware of the Shang Dynasty.

3-9-2

3-9-2*

3-9-3*

3-9-3

3-9-3 Four-ram bronze *zun* Wine container, Shang period, height 58.6 cm, mouth diameter 44.4 cm; unearthed in 1938 in Ningxiang County, Hunan Province.

3-9-4 Bronze human head Sacrificial object, Shang period, height 37.5 cm; unearthed in 1986 at Sanxingdui, Guanghan County, Sichuan Province. It is the image of a sorcerer of the Shu people in west China.

3-9-5 Bronze mirror Relic of the period between Qijia and Kayue cultures, 14.6 cm in diameter, 0.15 cm thick along the edge, knob 0.5 cm high; said to have been unearthed in Gansu Province. This is one of the very few early bronze mirrors of China's Bronze Age.

3-9-4

3-9-5

Warring States Period

Usurpation of government power in the state of Qi by the Tian family and division of Jin into the three states of Han, Zhao and Wei marked the beginning of the Warring States Period in Chinese history. It was a period of unprecedentedly fierce wars of annexation, but also one of rapid growth in the economy and culture. The feudal system was in a dominant position by this time, and the new mode of production it established was in an ascendant stage. The rulers of the feudal states, to maintain themselves and contend with each other in wars of annexation, undertook reforms to develop and strengthen their economy and military power. The new social system and economic development promoted the emergence of new ideas and new schools of thought to meet the needs of reform, resulting in a lively situation with "a hundred schools of thought contending." In the realm of art there was also unprecedented vitality and enthusiasm. Medicine and the natural sciences also made new progress with discoveries and inventions outstripping the rest of the world. The increase in economic and cultural exchanges between different regions and the consequent integration of different nationalities laid the foundation for the eventual establishment of a unified, multinational country.

Coexistence of Seven Powers

During the Warring States Period, the seven largest states – Qi, Chu, Yan, Han, Zhao, Wei and Qin – waged fierce wars with each other, grabbing land and cities. To strengthen themselves economically and militarily, they had to carry out social reforms. Qin, in the west, became more and more powerful as a result of its comparatively thorough reforms, and in the course of time was able to annex the six states in the east.

4-1-1 Bronze dagger-axe used by Zheng Youku
Weapon of Han, Warring States Period, length 25.2 cm, arm 11.2 cm; unearthed in 1971 at Baimiaofan Village, Xinzheng County, Henan Province.

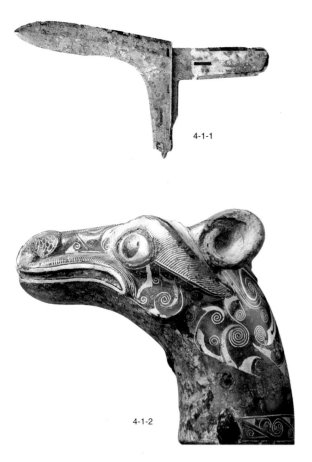

4-1-1

4-1-2

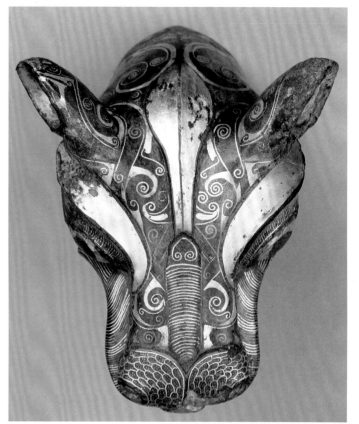

4-1-3

4-1-4 Pottery *hu* with animal-shaped ears painted in red Wine container of Yan, Warring States Period, height 70.2 cm; unearthed in 1964 in Songyuan Village, Changping County, Beijing.

4-1-5 Zihezi's bronze *fu* Measuring device of Qi, Warring States Period, height 38.5 cm, mouth diameter 22.3 cm; unearthed in 1857 at Lingshanwei, Jiao County, Shandong Province. Tests show that its volume is 2,040 ml. On the body of the *fu* is an inscription of 9 lines, recording Zihezi's promulgation of standards of volume.

4-1-2 Bronze horsehead with gold and silver inlay Ornament on shaft of carriage, relic of Wei, Warring States Period, height 8.8 cm, length 13.7 cm; unearthed at Guwei Village, Hui County, Henan Province. It is a typical example of gold and silver inlaid ornaments of the Warring States Period.

4-1-3 Bronze *hu* cast by the adopted son of the Squire of Linghu Wine container of Han, Warring States Period, height 46.5 cm. On the neck of the *hu* is an inscription of 50 characters in 23 lines, a eulogy by the adopted son of the Squire of Linghu to mark the casting of the vessel.

4-1-4

4-1-5

4-1-6

4-1-7

4-1-8

4-1-9

4-1-6 Bronze lamp with human figure
Relic of Qi, Warring States Period, height 21.3 cm, plate diameter 11.5 cm; unearthed in 1957 in Zhucheng County, Shandong Province. The lamp consists of a human figure standing on a coiled dragon and holding in each hand a branch with a plate on top. The plates are attached to the branches by tenon and mortise and can be freely removed.

4-1-7 Bronze tripod of Xiong Han, King of Chu Chu ritual vessel, Warring States Period, height 55.6 cm; said to have been unearthed in 1933 at Zhujiaji, Shou County, Anhui Province.

Inscriptions record that the vessel was cast by Xiong Han, King You of Chu.

4-1-8 Bronze *lei* Wine container of Chu, Warring States Period, height 37 cm; recovered in 1954 in Tai'an, Shandong Province.

4-1-9 Bronze dagger-axe with brocade design
Weapon of Chu, Warring States Period, length 24 cm; said to have been unearthed in Changsha, Hunan Province. Both sides of the weapon are decorated with exquisitely carved diamond-shaped brocade patterns.

4-1-10 Bronze crouching ox with silver inlay
Chu relic, Warring States Period, length 10 cm; unearthed in 1956 in Shou County, Anhui Province. Under the belly is an inscription saying that it belonged to the Chu royal family.

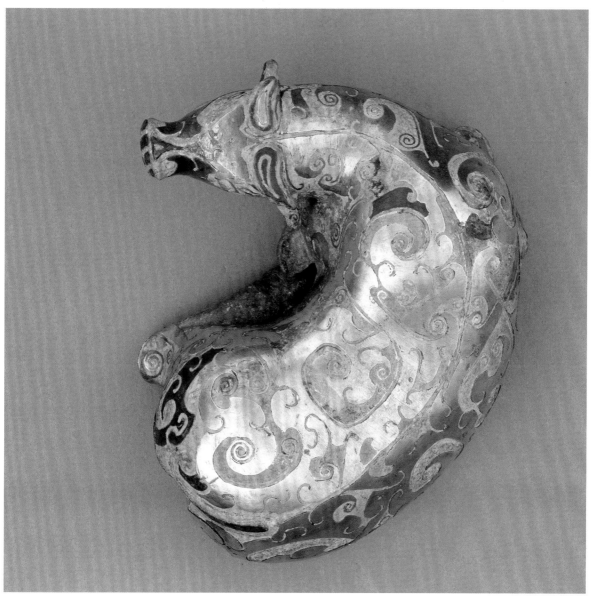

4-1-10

4-1-11

4-1-11 Bronze mirror with figures of warriors fighting beasts Qin relic, Warring States Period, 10.4 cm in diameter; unearthed in 1975 from a Qin tomb at Shuihudi, Yunmeng County, Hubei Province.

4-1-12 Lu Buwei's "Fourth Year" bronze dagger-axe head Qin weapon, Warring States Period, length 21 cm; unearthed in 1957 in Changsha, Hunan Province. Inscriptions on the *nei* (part that joins the head to handle) say that it was used by Lu Buwei.

4-1-12

Economy of the Warring States Period

The establishment of the feudal system and the reforms undertaken by various states led to rapid development on the economic front. The wide use of iron tools and extensive construction of water conservancy projects helped promote the growth of agriculture. Along with the rapid development of handicrafts and commerce, cities that were once political and military citadels became industrial and commercial metropolises and economic centers.

4-2-1

4-2-2

4-2-3

4-2-1 Mold for casting two sickles simultaneously Yan tool, Warring States Period, length 32 cm, width 11.3 cm; unearthed in 1953 at Gudonggou, Xinglong County, Hebei Province. Near the handles of the sickles are two characters, *You Lin* in pinyin transliteration, the title of the official in charge of casting.

4-2-2 Table showing the compositions of six kinds of bronze objects The ancient writing *Artificers' Record* contains a summary of bronze making in China during the pre-Qin period. It lists the proportions of different metals in six kinds of bronze objects.

4-2-3 Bronze mirror with coiled-dragon openwork Chu relic, Warring States Period, 20.5 cm in diameter; unearthed in 1976 at Zhangjiashan, Jiangling County, Hubei Province.

4-2-4 Bronze *lian*, openwork with animal design   Chu relic, Warring States Period, length 14 cm; unearthed in 1957 at Changtai Pass, Xinyang, Henan Province.

4-2-5 Bronze *jian*   Ice and wine container of Zeng, Warring States Period, 76 cm long on each side and 63.2 cm high; unearthed in 1977 from Tomb No.1 at Leigudun, Sui County, Hubei Province. It is a square box with a square flask inside. The flask was to hold wine, and the box ice cubes to keep the wine cool.

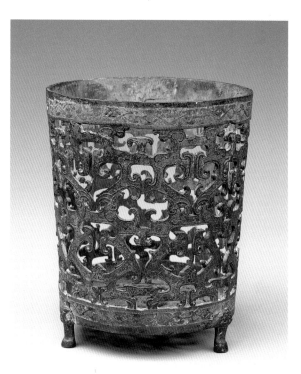

4-2-4

4-2-5

4-2-6

4-2-6 Bronze jar Wine container of Zeng, Warring States Period, length 124.5 cm, mouth diameter 48.4 cm; unearthed in 1977 from Tomb No.1 at Leigudun, Sui County, Hubei Province. It was a large wine container used in the house of Marquis Yi of Zeng.

4-2-7 Ejun Qi's gold-inlaid bronze tallies Relic of Chu, Warring States Period, length 30.9 cm and 29.6 cm, width 7.1 cm and 7.3 cm respectively; unearthed in 1957 from Qiujia Garden, Shou County, Anhui Province. The tallies, permits for land and water transportation, were given to Ejun Qi by King Huai of Chu.

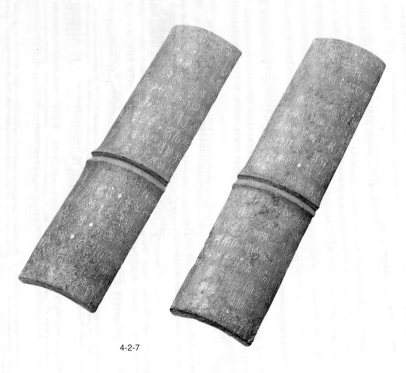

4-2-7

4-2-8

4-2-8 Small black lacquer table with vermilion designs Furniture of the Warring States Period, height 40.5 cm, length 57 cm, width 10 cm.

4-2-9 Lacquered cup with ears Wine cup of Zeng, Warring States Period, height 4.2 cm; unearthed in 1978 from Tomb No.1 at Leigudun, Sui County, Hubei Province.

4-2-10 Fragments of woven fabric Chu relics, Warring States Period; unearthed in 1951-52 in Changsha, Hunan Province.

4-2-9

4-2-10

4-2-11 Porcelain pot with dragon handle
Wine container of Chu, Warring States
Period, height 18 cm, mouth diameter 7 cm;
unearthed in 1955 at Li Zhu, Shaoxing,
Zhejiang Province. It is one of the best
examples of China's primitive celadons.
4-2-12 Ganyou silver ladle   Relic of Warring
States Period, height 3.7 cm; said to have been
unearthed at Jin Village, Luoyang, Henan
Province.

4-2-13

4-2-15

4-2-15 Glass ball Ornament of the Warring States Period, 6.3 cm in diameter. It is made of glaze (primitive glass) inlaid with colored material.

4-2-16 Half of a tile-end with ogre mask design Building material of Yan, Warring States Period, 9.8 cm high, 19.8 cm in diameter; unearthed in 1930 from the ruins of the Yan capital, Xiadu, in Yi County, Hebei Province.

4-2-17 Semicylindrical tile with *fufu* patterns Building material of Yan, Warring States Period, length 90.2 cm, diameter 36 cm; said to have been unearthed from the ruins of Xiadu, Yi County, Hebei Province. *Fufu* is a pattern used to embroider ceremonial robes in ancient times.

4-2-14

4-2-13 Silver belt fastener with gold plating, jade inlay, and glazed pearls Wei relic, Warring States Period, length 18.4 cm; unearthed in 1951 from Tomb No.1, Guwei Village, Hui County, Henan Province.

4-2-14 Jade pendant with cloud-and-animal design Wei ornament, Warring States Period, length 20.5 cm; unearthed in 1951 from Tomb No.1, Guwei Village, Hui County, Henan Province.

4-2-16

4-2-17

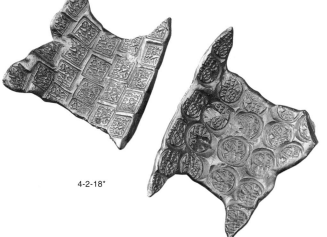

4-2-18

4-2-18*

4-2-20

4-2-18 Currencies of the Warring States Period Copper coins and gold were the chief currencies of the Warring States Period. Copper currencies were divided into *bu* (cloth), *dao* (knife-shaped), *yuan* (round) and *bei* (shell). *Bu* and *bei* coins were not actually made of cloth and shell. *Bu* was circulated mainly in the states of Han, Zhao and Wei. *Dao* was used chiefly in the states of Qi, Yan and Zhao. *Yuan* was used mainly in East and West Zhou and Qin, and in the territories of Zhao and Wei along the Yellow River. *Bei* was used mainly in Chu. Gold currency was circulated mainly in Chu and was of two kinds, coins and blocks. Most gold blocks bore stamped imprints.

4-2-19 Scale and ring weights Chu weighing apparatus, Warring States Period, beam 24 cm long, with nine ring weights; unearthed in 1954 at Zuojiagongshan, Changsha, Hunan Province.

4-2-20 Bronze scales with Chinese character for "king" Chu weighing scales, Warring States Period, length 23.1 cm and 23.15 cm respectively; said to have been unearthed in Shou County, Anhui Province.

4-2-19

Science, Culture and Contention of a Hundred Schools

The establishment of the feudal system, economic growth and intensified wars for unification led to the development of science and culture and to great activity on the academic and ideological fronts. They also helped to elucidate and promote many philosophical theories and ideas, creating a lively situation of "a hundred schools of thought contending." During the Warring States Period, new achievements were made in such disciplines as astronomy, optics, agronomy and medicine, which were in a leading position in the world at the time. Important achievements were also made in literature, history, painting, and music and dance.

4-3-1 Brush pen Chu writing implement, Warring States Period, length 21.2 cm; unearthed in 1954 at Zuojiagongshan, Changsha, Hunan Province.

4-3-2 Bronze chimes Chu musical instrument, Warring States Period, set of 13 chimes, height from 30.5 to 13 cm; unearthed in 1957 at Changtaiguan, Xinyang, Henan Province.

4-3-3 Stone chimes Wei musical instrument, Warring States Period, set of 10 chimes, length from 72.9 to 29 cm; unearthed in 1957 at Houchuan, Shaan County, Henan Province.

Principal schools of the Warring States Period

School	Chief Representative (s)
Mohists	Mo Di
Confucianists	Meng Ke, Xun Kuang
Taoists	Zhuang Zhou
Legalists	Li Kui, Shang Yang, Han Fei
Logicians	Hui Shi, Gongsun Long
Yin-Yang	Zou Yan
Political strategists	Zhang Yi, Su Qin
Military strategists	Sun Bin, Wu Qi
Agriculturists	Xu Xing
Eclectics	Lu Buwei

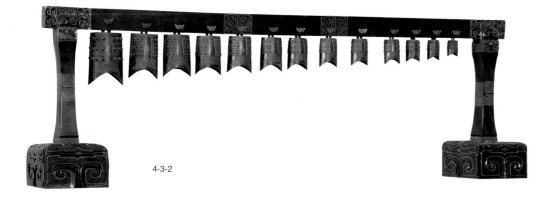

4-3-2

4-3-3

4-3-1

Peripheral Ethnics During the Warring States Period

Among the minorities living in the northern and northeastern parts of the country during the Warring States Period were the Linhu, Loufan, and Donghu tribes, nomads who settled wherever there was grass and water, and the Eastern Yi tribes whose main occupations were farming and stock raising. The Yue tribes inhabited what are now southern Jiangsu Province, Zhejiang, Fujian, Jiangxi, southern Hunan, Guangdong and Guangxi provinces. Comprising numerous branches, they were collectively called the Baiyue (Hundred Yues). Most of the minority peoples in the southwest boast long cultural traditions in their own localities. Some, however, migrated from Gansu and Qinghai in the northwest. The Shu and Ba peoples, in what is now Sichuan Province, assimilated much from the cultures of Qin and Chu, but the bronze cultures of Yunnan and Guizhou possessed marked local characteristics. As the links between the minority peoples and the peoples in various feudal states increased, they influenced each other, merged, and, in some cases, the minorities were assimilated into the feudal states.

4-4-1

4-4-2

4-4-1 Gold ornamental plate with design of tigers fighting bulls Hu ornament of the Warring States Period, length 12.7 cm, width 7.4 cm, weight 237.625 grams; unearthed in 1972 in Hanggin Banner, Ih Ju League of the Inner Mongolia Autonomous Region.

4-4-2 Boot-shaped bronze battle-axe Baiyue weapon, Warring States Period, length 8.5 cm, blade width 13.7 cm; unearthed in 1974 at Yinshanling, Pingle County, Guangxi Zhuang Autonomous Region.

4-4-3 Bronze *zheng* with image of tiger Shu relic, Warring States Period, height 39.3 cm; said to have been unearthed in Xinjin County, Sichuan Province.

4-4-4 Bronze rhinoceros-shaped belt hook inlaid with gold Ba relic, Warring States Period, length 17.5 cm, height 6.5 cm; unearthed in 1954 in Zhaohua County, Sichuan Province.

4-4-3

4-4-4

Qin, Western Han and Eastern Han (221BC—AD220)

Qin Unifies China

By the late Warring States Period, along with the rapid development of the economy and culture, unification of the country had become an irreversible historical trend. During the ten years from 230 to 221 BC, Yingzheng, the king of Qin, annexed the six states of Han, Zhao, Wei, Chu, Yan and Qi, ending a long period of divisive rule by feudal lords.

After conquering the six states, King Yingzheng styled himself the " first emperor." He set up a system of prefectures and counties in the country; unified the written language, currency, weights and measures; and built the Great Wall and many roadways. Thus the first unified, multinational feudal country with centralized power in Chinese history was established – an accomplishment of great significance to the development of China's political system.

However, the Qin court exacted heavy unpaid labor and instituted severe forms of punishment, which led to China's first large-scale peasant uprising, launched by Chen Sheng and Wu Guang in 209 BC. In 206 BC, a rebel army led by Liu Bang attacked and occupied Xianyang, the capital of Qin, and overthrew the Qin Dynasty.

5-1-1

5-1-2

5-1-1 Annals on bamboo slips Qin relic, length 23.1-27.8 cm, width 0.5-0.8 cm; unearthed in 1975 from Qin Grave No.11 at Shuihudi, Yunmeng County, Hubei Province. The Annals, written on 53 slips, records major events in the 90 years from 306 BC, the 1st year of King Zhao of Qin's reign, to 217 BC, the 30th year of the First Emperor of Qin's reign, including important battles to annex the six states.

5-1-2 Terra-cotta warrior Qin funerary object, 190 cm tall; unearthed in 1974 from a pit of terra-cotta horses and warriors in the First Emperor's mausoleum in Lintong County, Shaanxi Province.

5-1-3 Portrait of the First Emperor of Qin

5-1-4 Tiger tally of Yangling Relic of Qin, 8.9 cm long, 2.1 cm wide, 3.4 cm high; made of bronze cast in the shape of a tiger and divided into two halves along the middle. An imperial order in 12 characters to a general in Yangling was inlaid in gold on both sides of the tiger. It reads in translation: "Tally for moving soldiers; the right half is in the emperor's hands, the left half at Yangling." The order would not be considered valid unless the two halves matched.

5-1-3

5-1-4

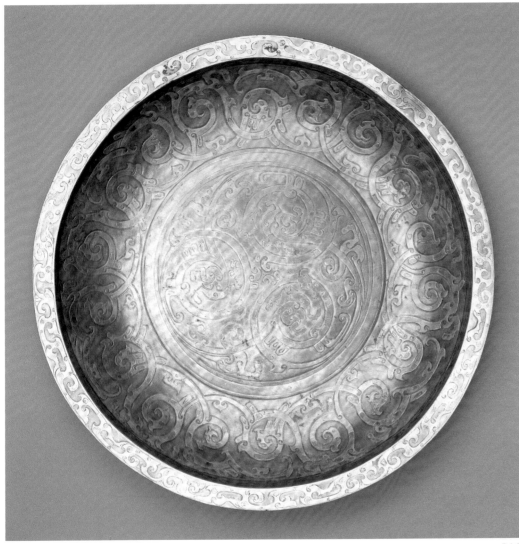

5-1-5*

5-1-5 Silver plate with gilt dragon designs Relic of Qin, rim diameter 37 cm, height 5.5 cm; unearthed in 1979 at Wotu Village, Zibo, Shandong Province. Under the rim were three characters meaning thirty-third year, i.e. the 33rd year of the reign of the First Emperor. The inscription shows that the plate was used in the emperor's Xianyang Palace.

5-1-5

5-1-6 Brick with 12 characters in small seal script   Relic of Qin, 30.8 cm long, 26.7 cm wide, 4 cm thick. The characters inscribed on the brick say: "Loyal subjects every where; bumper harvest every year; no hungry men on the streets."

5-1-6

5-1-7

5-1-7*

5-1-7 Eight-catty bronze *quan*   Weight of Qin, height 5.5 cm, base diameter 9.8 cm, weight 2,063.5 grams. Inscribed on the body of the *quan* are two characters that read in translation, "Eight catties." Also inscribed on the *quan* is an imperial edict on the unification of weights and measures issued in the 26th year of the reign of the First Emperor.

5-1-8 Big tile-end   Relic of Qin, diameter about 40 cm; unearthed in 1956 at the site of the Mausoleum of the First Emperor, Lintong, Shaanxi Province.

5-1-8

The Powerful and Prosperous Western Han

In its early years, learning from the rapid downfall of the Qin regime, the Western Han Dynasty adopted a policy of letting the people relax and recuperate. As a result, the sagging social economy was able to revive. At the same time, with the crackdown on local separatist forces, the unity of the country was further strengthened. After Liu Che, Emperor Wu of Han, succeeded to the throne, the government continued to weaken the power of local regimes. It stationed envoys in the Western Regions, launched large-scale counterattacks against the Xiongnu, enforced state management of the salt and iron industry, decreed a state monopoly on the mintage of coins, and proscribed all non- Confucian schools of thought by espousing Confucianism as the orthodox state ideology. Thus centralized state power was strengthened, the unified multinational feudal country was further consolidated, and Western Han reached the zenith of its rule.

In the late Western Han, struggles for annexation of land intensified, more and more people were forced into slavery, and social crises became increasingly severe. Capitalizing on the un-stable situation, Wang Mang, a maternal relative of the imperial family, proclaimed himself emperor in AD 8 and established the Xin Dynasty to replace the Han. To extricate the country from its predicament, he carried out a number of reforms including currency reforms, but all of them failed. Peasant uprisings broke out in both north and south China, and in AD 23 the short-lived Xin Dynasty was overthrown. During the Western Han Dynasty, great progress was made in the social economy. Iron farm tools were widely used, ox-plowing was popularized, plowing techniques improved, and large water conservancy projects were built. The handicraft industry was highly developed in both scale and technique. Its products included brightly colored silks and satins and exquisite lacquerware. Commerce and communication also developed, so did trade with foreign countries.

5-2-1 Tile-end inscribed with characters "Han unified the country" Relic of Western Han, diameter 17.5 cm; unearthed from the ruins of the Han city Chang'an at Xi'an, Shaanxi Province.

5-2-2 Colored figurines of infantrymen Relics of Western Han, height 48-50 cm; unearthed in 1965 at Yangjiawan, Xianyang, Shaanxi Province.

5-2-1

5-2-2

5-2-3

5-2-4

5-2-3 Tile-end with the characters "Heaven's mandate for Chanyu" Relic of Western Han, diameter 17.1 cm; unearthed in 1955 at Zhaowan, Baotou, Inner Mongolia Autonomous Region. Chanyu was a title used by a Xiongnu chieftain.

5-2-4 Big iron plowshare and plowshare with soil-digger Relics of Western Han, unearthed in 1955 at Sandaohao, Liaoyang, Liaoning Province and in 1967 at Yaodian, Xianyang, Shaanxi Province respectively.

5-2-5 Jade clothes sewn with gold thread Grave clothes of Western Han, 182 cm long; unearthed in 1973 from Han Tomb No.40 at Bajiaolang Village, Ding County, Hebei Province. They were worn by Liu Xiu, Prince Huai of Zhongshan, and consisted of 1,203 pieces of jade, sewn together with 2,567 grams of gold thread.

5-2-5*

5-2-

5-2-6 Painted bronze lamp in the shape of a wild goose Western Han, 53 cm tall; unearthed in 1985 at Zhao Shibazhuang, Shuo County, Shanxi Province. The lamp plate and chimney can be moved to adjust the light and keep away the wind. The fish and the neck and body of the wild goose are hollow and connected to each other; they hold the smoke and ashes. All parts of the lamp are detachable.

5-2-7 Bronze rhino-shaped *zun* inlaid with gold and silver cloud designs Wine vessel of Western Han, 58.1 cm long, 34.1 cm tall; unearthed in 1963 in Xinping County, Shaanxi Province.

5-2-6

5-2-6*

5-2-7

5-2-8

5-2-8 Embroidery of thin, tough silk with cornel design Western Han, unearthed in 1972 from a Han tomb at Mawangdui, Changsha, Hunan Province.

5-2-9 Painted pottery jar with dragon-and-tiger design Western Han, height 48.5 cm, mouth diameter 18.8 cm, base diameter 18.1 cm; unearthed in 1953 from a Han tomb at Shaogou, Luoyang, Henan Province.

5-2-10 Ancient vehicle made of wood and bamboo Funerary object of Western Han, length 106 cm; unearthed between 1951 and 1952 at Wujialing, Changsha, Henan Province.

5-2-9

5-2-10

5-2-11

5-2-11 Bronze mirror with inscription "Second Year of Shijianguo" Xin Dynasty, diameter 16 cm, thickness 0.4 cm. The earliest mirror with date discovered in China.

5-2-12 Coins used during Wang Mang's Xin Dynasty Minted during Wang Mang's reign, they are called: *huobu*, *qidao*-500, *yidaoping*-5000, *buquan*, *huoquan*, *xiaoquanzhi*-1, *yaoquan*-10, *youquan*-20, *zhongquan*-30, *zhuangquan*-40, and *daquan*- 50.

5-2-13 Coin with inscription "Guo Bao Jin Kui Zhi Wan" Xin Dynasty, length 6.2 cm, weight 41.7 grams. The characters "Guo Bao Jin Kui" mean national treasure and "Zhi Wan" mean "worth 10,000 *qian* of gold."

5-2-11*

5-2-13

5-2-12

Expansion of Despotic Forces in the Eastern Han

After the downfall of the Xin Dynasty, Liu Xiu, a member of the Han royal family, re-established the Han Dynasty in AD 25, with its capital at Luoyang to the east of the former Western Han's capital Xi'an; hence his dynasty was known in history as the Eastern Han. It was established with the help of the country's powerful landlords and therefore represented their interests. These landlords and their clans often held high official posts from generation to generation. They had large numbers of "disciples", "loyal former subordinates" and private armies, and controlled political power at both central and local levels.

Political corruption in the late Eastern Han resulted in severe social crises. Zhang Jue of Julu founded a secret religious sect named Taiping Tao (Doctrine of Justice) to organize the peasants. He spread the idea that "Blue Heaven" (referring to the Eastern Han government) had "passed away" and it was time for "Yellow Heaven" (the Yellow Turbans) to take over. After long years of preparation, he launched in AD 184 the Yellow Turbans Uprising, which seriously undermined the rule of the Eastern Han.

The Eastern Han period saw continued development of the social economy. Ox-plowing was further popularized, iron farm tools were widely used, and construction of water conservancy projects made great progress. Iron-smelting and handicraft production such as the making of pottery and porcelain also progressed. The manors administered by powerful landlords had the characteristics of a self-sufficient economy. Agriculture was their main line, but animal husbandry, handicraft and commerce were also undertaken.

5-3-1 Green-glazed pottery model of a tower-pavilion Burial object of Eastern Han, 144 cm tall; unearthed in 1956 at Guhe, Gaotang County, Shandong Province.
5-3-2 Brick relief of harvesting, fishing and hunting Eastern Han tomb chamber decoration, height 36 cm, width 42 cm; unearthed in 1954 at Yangzishan, Chengdu, Sichuan Province.
5-3-3 Brick relief of a brewery Eastern Han tomb chamber decoration, height 28.4 cm, width 38.3 cm; unearthed in 1954 in Pengshan County, Sichuan Province.

5-3-1

5-3-2

5-3-3

5-3-4

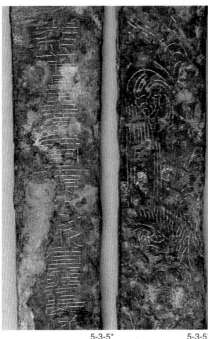

5-3-5*   5-3-5**

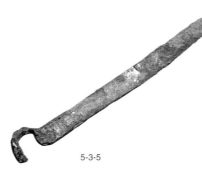

5-3-5

1956 at Honglou, Tongshan County, Xuzhou, Jiangsu Province.

5-3-7 Brocade sock for "prolonging life and benefiting one's sons and grandsons" Relic of Eastern Han, length 43.5 cm, width 17.3 cm; unearthed in 1959 at Niya, Minfeng County, Xinjiang Uygur Autonomous Region.

5-3-7

5-3-4 Rubbing from a stone carving of a scene of iron smelting (section) Eastern Han tomb chamber decoration, height of stone surface 80 cm, width 144 cm; unearthed in 1930 in Teng County, Shandong Province.
5-3-5 Iron *shu*-knife with gold inlay A knife for trimming bamboo slips, Eastern Han, length 18.5 cm, width 1.5 cm; unearthed in 1957 at Tianhuishan, Chengdu, Sichuan Province. On one side of the blade is a gold-inlaid phoenix design; on the other side, a gold-inlaid inscription saying it was made in AD 184 by a government handicraft workshop in Guanghan, Sichuan Provoince.
5-3-6 Rubbing from a stone engraving of silk weavers (section) Tomb chamber decoration of Eastern Han, height of stone surface 99 cm, width 234 cm; unearthed in

5-3-6

5-3-8

5-3-9*

5-3-8 Green-glazed pottery water pavilion
Funerary object of Eastern Han, height 54.5 cm; unearthed at Sanlixi Village, Xinzhuzhen, Xi'an, Shaanxi Province.
5-3-9 Pottery boat Funerary object of Eastern Han, height 16 cm, length 54 cm; unearthed in 1954 at Xianlie Road, Guangzhou, Guangdong Province.

5-3-9

Peripheral Minority Nationalities of the Han Dynasty

The unity of the country during the Western and Eastern Han dynasties helped strengthen ties and mutual influence between the Han and various minority nationalities. Besides the populous Han nationality, which lived mostly in the Central Plains, the principal minority nationalities at the time were the Xiongnu in the north, the Wuhuan and Xianbei in the northeast, the Qiang in the northwest, various tribes in the Western Regions, the Baiyue in the south and southeast, and the southwestern Yi in the southwest. The people of all these nationalities created cultures of their own, contributing to the historical development of the multinational country.

5-4-1

5-4-2*

5-4-2

5-4-3

5-4-4

5-4-1 Bronze buckle with figurines of three musicians Ornament of Western Han, length 4.5 cm, width 1.9 cm; unearthed in 1956 in Jungar Banner, Inner Mongolia Autonomous Region.

5-4-2 Bronze seal with eight characters Relic of Eastern Han, height 2.9 cm, length of each side 2.3 cm; unearthed in 1979 at Upper Sunjiazhai, Datong Hui-Tu Autonomous County, Qinghai Province. The characters show the allegiance of the Xiongnu chief Guiyi to the Han.

5-4-3 Bronze plate with images of mounted warriors Belt ornament of Western Han, length 11.1 cm, width 8.4 cm; unearthed in 1956 at Xichagou, Xifeng County, Liaoning Province.

5-4-4 Gilded bronze plate with divine-animal motif Relic of Han, length 11.3 cm, width 7.2 cm; unearthed in 1980 at Laoheshen, Yushu County, Jilin Province.

5-4-5 Bronze knife with sheep-head decoration
Relic of Western Han, length 23.3 cm, width 3.9 cm;
unearthed in 1959 at Chabuhahe, Xinyuan County,
Xinjiang Uygur Autonomous Region.

5-4-6 Four joined earthern jars Relics of Western
Han, length 17.5 cm, height 10.1 cm; unearthed in 1957
at Overseas Chinese New Village in Guangzhou,
Guangdong Province.

5-4-7 Bronze drum with Han 5-*zhu* coin motif Relic
of Han, diameter 90 cm, height 57.2 cm, weight 75.4
kg; unearthed in 1954 in Cenxi County, Guangxi
Zhuang Autonomous Region. The drum is decorated
with 5-*zhu* motifs on the top and all over the body,
suggesting cultural mergence between the Han and
minority nationalities in south China.

5-4-6

5-4-5

5-4-7

5-4-8 King of Dian's gold seal Relic of Western Han,
1.8 cm high, side 2.3 cm long, weight 89.5 grams;
unearthed in 1956 at Shizhaishan, Jinning County,
Yunnan Province. In 109 BC Emperor Wu of Han gave
the king of Dian a seal of authority to continue his rule
over the Dian people. The discovery of this gold seal
confirms what is recorded in history books.

**5-4-9 Bronze cowrie container with tiger-shaped ears
and statuettes of seven buffaloes** Relic of Western Han,
height 43.5 cm, bottom diameter 21.8 cm; unearthed at
Shizhaishan, Jinning County, Yunnan Province.

5-4-8   5-4-8*

5-4-9

Science and Culture of the Han Dynasty

Brilliant achievements were made in science and culture during the Han Dynasty, achievements that rivaled the dynasty's highly developed feudal economy and placed China in the forefront of the world's ancient civilized countries. People first learnt how to make rough plant fiber paper from waste linen during the Western Han. By the Eastern Han, Cai Lun, improving on existing techniques and widening the source of raw material, made a finer grade of plant fiber paper which people called "Marquis Cai's paper." In astronomy, the world's earliest recording of sun spots and nova was made in China during the Western Han, and Zhang Heng of the Eastern Han invented a seismograph, the first instrument of its kind in the world. In medicine, Zhang Zhongjing laid the foundation for dialectical treatment in Chinese traditional medicine and Hua Tuo was the first surgeon in the world to use general drug anaesthesia in major operations. During the reign of Emperor Wu, fifth Western Han emperor, Confucianism became predominant and Confucian classics were made the official philosophy, but Wang Chong of the Eastern Han expounded and espoused materialist ideology. In religion, Taoism,

5-5-1

5-5-1 Fufeng paper Western Han, remaining part 7.4 cm long, 6.8 cm wide; unearthed in 1978 in Fufeng County, Shaanxi Province.
5-5-2 Seismograph (model) Reproduced by the National Museum of Chinese History.
5-5-3 Rubbing of a stone engraving showing acupuncture treatment (section) Eastern Han, length of original stone 94.5 cm, width 91.5 cm, thickness 24 cm; unearthed at Liangcheng, Weishan County,

5-5-3

which originated from sorcery and supernatural divination, took shape in the late Western Han and flourished during the Eastern Han; while exotic Buddhism from India was introduced into China in the late Western Han. Translation of Buddhist scriptures began during the Eastern Han, Buddhist temples were set up, and Buddhism gradually spread. In the arts and letters, the Han Dynasty boasted a great number of excellent prose writings, including rhymed prose, and folk songs rich in content and lively in style. Emperor Wu created a music bureau, called *yuefu* in Chinese, specially to collect folk songs. Later, during the Eastern Han, poems with five characters to a line in imitation of the *yuefu* style appeared. *Records of the Historian* by Sima Qian of the Western Han was China's first systematized and comprehensive history book, a model historical record of feudalism for later periods. *History of the Han Dynasty* by Ban Gu of the Eastern Han initiated the writing of dynastic histories. Paintings and sculptures of Han Dynasty were realistic and of high artistic level. Absorbing foreign elements, music, dance and acrobatics all became richer and more colorful.

5-5-2

5-5-5*

5-5-4

Shandong Province. The stone engraving consists of three parts. The middle part depicts a creature with a human face and a bird's body, holding a needle to apply acupuncture to his patient.

5-5-4 Fragment of tablet of "Xiping Stone Classics" Eastern Han, 45 cm high. In 175, the fourth year of the Xiping reign of Eastern Han emperor Ling, Cai Yong and others made handwritten copies in official script of seven Confucian classics: the *Book of Songs*, *Book of History*, *Book of Changes*, *Book of Rites*, *Spring and Autumn Annals*, *Spring and Autumn Annals with Commentary by Gongyang Gao*, and *Analects of Confucius*. They were engraved on 46 stone tablets in the Imperial College in Luoyang, and are the earliest governmental standard versions of the seven classics in China.

5-5-5 Storytelling to the accompaniment of a drum (clay figurine) Funerary object of Eastern Han, 56 cm tall; unearthed in 1957 at Tianhuishan, Chengdu, Sichuan Province.

5-5-5

5-5-7*

5-5-7

5-5-6

5-5-6 Green glazed pottery stage Funerary object of Eastern Han, 99 cm high; unearthed in 1976 at Dawangdian, Woyang, Anhui Province. This is a four-storied structure. The top floor is a drum tower. On the second floor is the stage, which has a backstage, an entrance and an exit. On the stage are figurines of five performers.

5-5-7 Watching acrobatics (brick engraving) Eastern Han, length 46 cm, width 40 cm, thickness 5.3 cm; unearthed in 1954 at Yangzishan, Chengdu, Sichuan Province.

The Silk Road; Economic and Cultural Exchanges with Foreign Countries in the Han Dynasty

A new situation emerged in economic and cultural exchanges with foreign countries during the Han Dynasty. Zhang Qian went to the Western Regions on two occasions as an imperial envoy during the reign of Emperor Wu, opening up a land route from Chang'an, the capital, to Central and Western Asia through the Hexi corridor (west of the Yellow River) and along the southern road of the Tianshan Range. Further west, the route linked the European and African continents. Through this route, the exquisitely made silk of China found its way to countries in the West and, in return, products from the West were introduced into China. This thoroughfare of interchange between East and West was called the Silk Road. Its opening enhanced cultural intercourse between the Han empire and its neighbors, and enriched the life of the people in both the East and the West, becoming a bridge to strengthen ties and friendship between the Chinese people and peoples in Central and Western Asia, as well as in Africa and Europe later on.

5-6-1

5-6-1 Mural showing Zhang Qian on his trip to the Western Regions Copied from an early Tang mural in Dunhuang.

5-6-2 Blue glass bowl Western Han, height 4.7 cm, rim diameter 10.5 cm; unearthed in 1954 at Hengzhigang, Guangzhou, Guangdong Province. This is the earliest Roman glass vessel unearthed in China.

5-6-2

Three Kingdoms, Western and Eastern Jin, Northern and Southern Dynasties (220—589)

This was a period of both disturbances and development in Chinese history, especially during the Three Kingdoms and the two Jin dynasties, when political struggles were acute and civil wars frequent. Ethnic minorities in the north entered the Central Plains and set up governments there. The result was a long period of confrontation between these minority regimes and regimes established by Han Chinese in the south. The economy in the south made some progress during this time, and the northern regimes accepted in varying degrees the Han political system and its culture. This was the beginning of a process of mergence between Han and minority cultures. China's contacts with foreign countries also became more frequent. Buddhist culture of the Western Regions, in particular, was introduced into China on a large scale, exerting a far-reaching influence on Chinese culture. Great progress was made in science and technology, and literature and art was at an important stage linking the past to the future.

Confrontation between Wei, Shu and Wu

Civil wars went on for many decades during the last years of Eastern Han. The killings were most tragic along the Yellow and Huai rivers, where people had to flee their homes and the economy was in ruins. Cao Cao, a warlord, in the name of supporting the Han emperor, defeated his rivals Lu Bu, Yuan Shao, Liu Biao, Han Sui and Ma Chao, and occupied the Yellow and Huai river valleys.

In 220 Cao Pi, his son, dethroned the Han emperor and established the kingdom of Wei, making Luoyang his capital. In 221 Liu Bei, a scion of the Han royal family, proclaimed himself emperor at Chengdu (in Sichuan Province) and reinstated the Han Dynasty; his regime was known in history as Shu or Shu-Han, Shu being another name for Sichuan. In 229 Sun Quan, a southern warlord, made himself emperor of Wu and moved his capital to Jianye (now Nanjing, Jiangsu Province). Thus the epoch of the Three Kingdoms was established.

Rulers of the Three Kingdoms made great efforts to revive their economies. They established a system of having garrison troops or peasants open up wasteland. In 221 and 227, the kingdom of Wei resumed the use of the Han five-*zhu* coins. Shu and Wu also issued large-denomination currencies to resolve their financial problems.

Celadon ware and bronze mirrors made in Wu were two representative handicraft products of the Three Kingdoms Period. The celadon ware had its unique pattern. Most bronze mirrors were decorated with immortal-and-animal designs and some with portraits of historical figures. All were exquisitely made.

6-1-1 Five-*zhu* coin Wei currency, Three Kingdoms Period, diameter 2.5 cm.

6-1-2 Bronze trigger mechanism of a crossbow Wei weapon, Three Kingdoms Period, length 11.9 cm; made in 241.

6-1-1

6-1-2

6-1-3

6-1-4

6-1-3 Pottery cup with side ears Wei, Three Kingdoms Period, length 11 cm; unearthed from Cao Zhi's tomb in Dong'a County, Shandong Province.

6-1-4 *Zhibai* five-*zhu* coins Shu currency, Three Kingdoms Period, diameter 2.6-2.8 cm.

6-1-5 Pottery figurine holding a dustpan Funerary object of Shu, Three Kingdoms Period, height 54 cm; unearthed in 1981 in Zhong County, Sichuan Province. Several dozen pottery figurines of laborers, dancers and singers were unearthed from the grave, suggesting that the grave occupant must have been a rich person.

6-1-6 Pottery courtyard Funerary object of Wu, Three Kingdoms Period, 54 cm long, 44 cm wide; unearthed in 1967 in Ezhou, Hubei Province. This clay courtyard was modelled on a real building. It is surrounded by a wall, has a room for guests in front, a main room facing south, and side rooms on the east and west. Built into the wall are a front gate with a tower above it and a rear gate. The four corner towers and the gate tower all serve as sentry posts. The original courtyard probably belonged to Sun Shu, a member of the royal family of Wu and governor of Wuchang.

6-1-5

6-1-6

6-1-7*

6-1-7

6-1-7 Celadon lamp Relic of Wu, Three Kingdoms Period, height 11.5 cm; unearthed in 1958 in Nanjing, Jiangsu Province. The main color agent is a small amount of iron in the glaze, which after being fired at a high temperature assumes a pale green or yellow green hue. In the middle of the lamp is a charmingly naive bear cub, carrying a plate that seems too heavy for him.

6-1-8

6-1-8 Sheep-shaped celadon *zun* Water vessel of Wu, Three Kingdoms Period, 30.5 cm long; unearthed in 1958 in Nanjing, Jiangsu Province. The *zun* is in the shape of a sheep coated with lustrous pale green glaze. The evenness of the coating reflects the high level of porcelain making techniques.

6-1-9 Bronze mirror with immortal-and-animal motif Relic of Wu, Three Kingdoms Period, diameter 12 cm, cast in the fifth year of the Yong'an reign. The mirror is decorated with a immortal-and-animal motif on the back.

6-1-9

Short Period of Unification Under the Western Jin

In 263 Wei conquered Shu. Two years later Sima Yan set up the Jin Dynasty (historically known as the Western Jin) to replace the Wei, with the capital remaining at Luoyang. In 280 Jin conquered Wu, reuniting the north and south. To consolidate imperial power, the Western Jin government granted administrative and military powers at both central and local levels to princes of the royal family. This, however, resulted in disturbances. After killing members of the Yang and Jia families, relatives of court ladies who held power behind the throne, the princes began fighting and killing each other in a desperate struggle for power; palace coups evolved into large-scale warfare known in history as the "Disturbances of the Eight Princes." The Central Plains was again severely devastated, and the political and military power of the Western Jin regime was greatly weakened. The Xiongnu tribe in the north became strong, and in 308 Liu Yuan, a Xiongnu noble, proclaimed himself emperor of Han. His army occupied Luoyang and Chang'an successively, and in 316 conquered the Western Jin.

6-2-1 Porcelain male and female figurines
Funerary objects of Western Jin, standing female 23.5 cm tall, sitting male 20.5 cm tall; unearthed in 1964 in Nanjing, Jiangsu

6-2-3

6-2-3*

6-2-1

6-2-2

6-2-4

Province. The female figurine, stripped to the waist, was probably a slave. The male, dressed in the costume of an official, must be the image of a civil officer in feudal China.

6-2-2 Pottery figurines of swordsmen
Funerary objects of Western Jin, left 20 cm tall, right 17 cm tall; unearthed in 1955 in Changsha, Hunan Province. They are images of officers or soldiers in the Western Jin army.

6-2-3 Bronze seal carved with the characters for "Qin Jin Hu Wang" Relic of Western Jin, about 2.5 cm long on each side. This seal was given to an ethnic minority leader in north China by the Western Jin government. The characters "Qin Jin Hu Wang" mean that the minority leader was royal to Jin. "Hu" was a general term used in ancient China for ethnic tribes in the north. During the Wei and Jin periods, the main ethnic tribes in north China were the Xiongnu, Di, Qiang, Wuhuan, Xianbei and Jie.

6-2-4 Iron halberds Weapons of Western Jin, remaining parts 16.8 cm (left) and 23 cm (right) long; unearthed in 1953 from Zhou Chu's tomb in Yixing, Jiangsu Province. Zhou Chu was a man famous for his readiness to correct his mistakes. In 297, when a severe drought struck northwest China, two ethnic minorities there, the Di and Qiang, rebelled. Zhou Chu led an army of only 5,000 against the rebels, who totalled 70,000, and was killed in the fighting.

6-2-5 Celadon incense burner Western Jin, 19.5 cm high; unearthed in 1953 from Zhou Chu tomb in Yixing, Jiangsu Province.

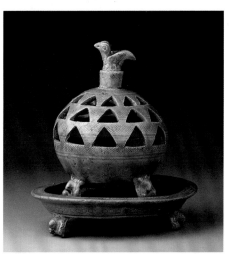

6-2-5

Further Development in the South

In 317 Sima Rui, a member of the royal family of the Western Jin, proclaimed himself emperor in the south, making Jiankang (today's Nanjing, Jiangsu Province) his capital. His regime is historically known as the Eastern Jin. In 383, the Eastern Jin defeated at Feishui an army of the powerful Former Qin, a minority regime in the north, and thereafter enjoyed a period of relative stability, which made possible a normal development of the economy in the south. In 420 Liu Yu, a general, usurped power, proclaimed himself emperor, and replaced the Eastern Jin with his Song Dynasty. Then in 479, 502 and 557, Generals Xiao Daocheng, Xiao Yan and Chen Baxian each in turn overthrew the established dynasty and replaced it with a new one, called the Qi, Liang and Chen respectively. These three dynasties, together with the Song set up by Liu Yu were collectively called the Southern Dynasties in Chinese history.

To escape the chaos of war, large numbers of people in the north had moved to the south during the late Western Jin, bringing with them laborers and advanced techniques of production. Porcelain, the representative handicraft product, was still largely made in the south; most such wares were simple in pattern and style, but there were some very exquisite objects.

6-3-1 Celadon pigsty, sheepfold and chicken-coop Funerary objects of Jin, diameter or length 10 cm, 6 cm and 14 cm respectively. Such enclosures for domestic animals were common in the Yangtze River delta during the Jin Dynasty. They reflect the stable agricultural economy and life at the time.

6-3-1

6-3-1*

6-3-1**

6-3-2 Black porcelain amphora with chicken-head spout Wine vessel of Eastern Jin, 15.6 cm high; unearthed in Zhenjiang, Jiangsu Province. During the Wei and Jin, people loved wine, good food and the pleasures of eating and drinking. They enjoyed the unrestraint of drunkenness, often using it as a way of escaping political persecution. Iron is the main coloring agent in black porcelain, same as in celadon. It reaches 4-8% of the glaze in the former but no more than 3% in the latter; hence their shades are different after firing.

6-3-2

6-3-3 Sheep-shaped celadon candle holder Eastern Jin, 14.7 cm high; unearthed in Zhenjiang, Jiangsu Province. This is a vessel with grayish green glaze and several dark brown spots, which are called underglaze color in ceramics. A little dark brown substance was added to the grayish green glaze before firing to produce this two-color porcelain vessel.

6-3-3

6-3-4

6-3-4*

6-3-4 Pottery figurine of a woman
Funerary object of Eastern Jin, 33.7 cm
high; unearthed in Nanjing, Jiangsu
Province

6-3-5 Celadon cup and saucer Tea set of
the Southern Dynasties, saucer 16 cm in
diameter, cup 12 cm in diameter;
unearthed in Fuzhou, Fujian Province.

**6-3-6 Celadon spittoon with stamped
decoration** Southern Dynasties, 12 cm
high; unearthed in Changsha, Hunan
Province.

6-3-5

6-3-6

Amalgamation of Nationalities in the North

The fall of the Western Jin in 316 was followed by a period of political fragmentation in the north, called the Sixteen States period. In 439 Northern Wei unified north China, a unity that lasted nearly 100 years until 534 when it split into the Eastern and Western Wei. Later these two Weis were replaced by the Northern Qi and Northern Zhou respectively. In 577, Northern Zhou conquered Northern Qi and the north was again united. Through long periods of productive activities and living together, the various nationalities in north China gradually merged, a process that accelerated the recovery and development of the region's economy. After the founding of the Sui Dynasty, north China became even more powerful. In 589 Sui conquered Chen, the last of the Southern Dynasties, ending a long period of confrontation between north and south.

6-4-1

6-4-2

6-4-3

6-4-4

6-4-1 Tile-end with characters "Da Qin Long Xing Hua Mou Gu Sheng" Former Qin, one of the Sixteen States, diameter 17.5 cm; unearthed in Yi County, Hebei Province. The characters on the tile-end say that the Former Qin's exploits were comparable to those of a sage.

6-4-2 *Daxia Zhenxing* coin Currency of Xia, one of the Sixteen States; diameter 2.3 cm, weight 2.2 g.

6-4-3 Stone dagoba built by Bai Shuangjie Northern Liang, one of the Sixteen States, remaining part 46 cm high, base diameter 21 cm; unearthed in Jiuquan, Gansu Province.

6-4-4 Tile-end with characters "Chuan Zuo Wu Qiong" Northern Wei, about 15.5 cm in diameter; unearthed in Datong, Shanxi Province. The four characters express the wish of the Northern Wei rulers to perpetuate their rule eternally.

6-4-5 Gold headdresses shaped like a horse head and ox head with antlers Relics of the Northern Dynasties, height 16.2cm and 17.5 cm, weight about 70g and 90g respectively; unearthed in 1981 in Darhan Muminggan Joint Banner, Inner Mongolia Autonomous Region.

6-4-5**

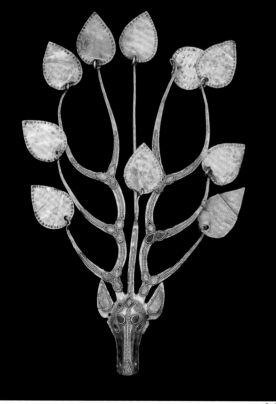

6-4-5

6-4-5*

6-4-6

6-4-6 Pottery mounted warriors Funerary objects of Northern Wei, about 38 cm high; unearthed in 1953 at Caochangpo, Xi'an, Shaanxi Province.

6-4-7 Pottery figure of a warrior Northern Wei, height 30.8 cm; unearthed in 1965 from Yuan Shao's tomb in Luoyang, Henan Province.

6-4-7

Site of the structural foundation of an old city of the Han-Wei period (reflection of negative vegetation)

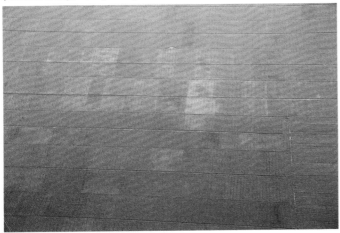

Structural foundation of the Yongningsi Pagoda and the sites around it in different seasons

6-4-8 Celadon *zun* with lotus design
Northern Wei, height 61.5 cm, mouth
diameter 16.4 cm; unearthed in 1948 from the
Feng Family cemetery in Jing County, Hebei
Province.

**6-4-9 Colored pottery figurines of civil and
military officers** Western Wei, height 40.2
cm and 38.9 cm respectively; unearthed in
1977 from a Western Wei tomb in Cuijiaying,
Hanzhong, Shaanxi Province.

6-4-8

6-4-9

6-4-10

6-4-10*

6-4-11

6-4-12

6-4-12 Yellow glazed porcelain flask with figures of dancers and musicians Northern Qi, height 20.5 cm, mouth diameter 5.1 cm, base diameter 10.1; unearthed in 1971 in Anyang, Henan Province.

6-4-13 Gilded saddlebows and stirrups Gaogouli, large saddlebow 50.5 cm wide, 25.4 cm high, stirrups about 26.8 cm high, 17.2 cm wide; unearthed in 1976 in Ji'an, Jilin Province.

6-4-10 Pottery figurine of a musician playing the pipa Northern Qi, height 28.2 cm; unearthed in 1973 from the Kudi Huiluo tomb in Shouyang County, Shanxi Province.

6-4-11 Pottery ox cart Funerary object of Northern Qi, cart 31.2 cm high, ox 23.2 cm high; unearthed in 1955 from Zhang Susu's tomb in Kuangpo, Taiyuan, Shanxi Province.

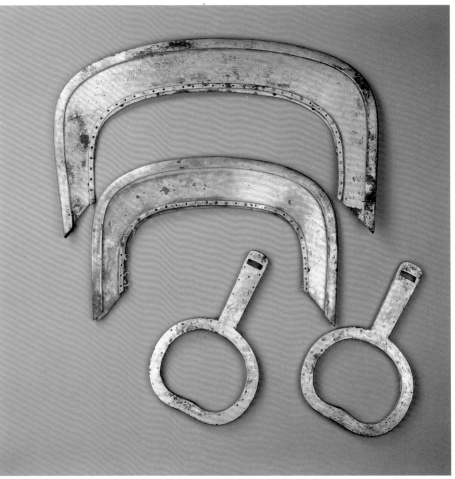

6-4-13

Cultural Exchange with Foreign Countries

China's trade interflow and cultural exchange with the West increased further during the Three Kingdoms, the two Jin dynasties, and the Northern and Southern Dynasties. Fa Xian, an eminent monk of Eastern Jin, was the first to go west to study Buddhist doctrines in the history of Chinese Buddhism. He was also the first to travel along the Silk Road to countries of Central and South Asia and return to China by sea.

6-5-2

6-5-1

6-5-1 Silver flask Relic of the third century, height 15.8 cm, rim diameter 7 cm, base diameter 5.4 cm; unearthed at Shangsunjiazhai, Datong Hui-Tu Autonomous County, Qinghai Province.

6-5-2 Gilded bronze goblet with inlaid decoration Relic of Byzantine, height 9.8 cm, mouth diameter 11.2 cm, base diameter 6.8 cm; unearthed in 1970 at the ruins of Northern Wei on the southern outskirts of Datong, Shanxi Province.

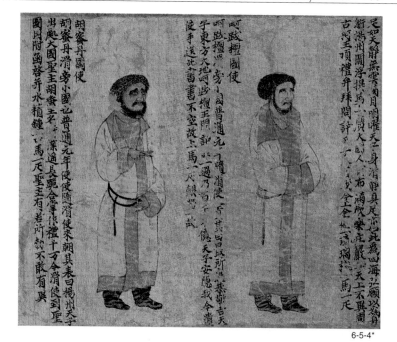

6-5-4*

6-5-3 Glass cup with netlike pattern Relic of Byzantine, height 6.7 cm, mouth diameter 10.3 cm, base diameter 4.5 cm; unearthed in 1948 from the Feng family cemetery of Northern Wei, Jing County, Hebei Province.

6-5-4 Scroll painting "Special Envoys" by Xiao Yi Copy made in the Song Dynasty, 25 x 198 cm. Xiao Yi (508- 554) was the seventh son of Xiao Yan, Emperor Wu of Liang. He excelled in painting and calligraphy. "Special Envoys" shows foreign envoys sent to China during the Liang period of the Southern Dynasties. At the side of each envoy is an

6-5-3

6-5-4**

inscription describing the country from which he came and China's relations with that country. The painting is a precious historical record of China's cultural relations with foreign countries in the sixth century.

6-5-4

Science and Technology, Art and Culture

The Three Kingdoms, two Jin dynasties, and Northern and Southern Dynasties were important periods in the development of China's science and culture. Numerous representative figures emerged in the fields of mathematics, astronomy, agriculture, medicine, iron smelting and foundry, and machine building, and their achievements had a far-reaching influence on later generations. In literature, history and geography, many important works that retained the fine traditions of the Han Dynasty were published. In calligraphy, painting and sculpture, talented artists appeared one after another and created beautiful works of timeless value. The fusion of nationalities, spread of Buddhism, and assimilation of exotic cultures further enriched the art and culture of this period, introducing new artistic styles of historic significance.

6-6-1 Model of the south-pointing carriage The model was made by the National Museum of Chinese History on the basis of the descriptions given in the *History of the Three Kingdoms* and *History of the Song Dynasty*.

6-6-2 Model of a Jin carriage with a mileage-recording drum The model was made by the National Museum of Chinese History on the basis of the *History of the Song Dynasty* and an Eastern Han stone engraving.

6-6-3 *Classic of Acupuncture and Moxibustion* by Huangfu Mi A Ming block-printed edition. In his *Classic of Acupuncture and Moxibustion* Huangfu Mi (215-282), an expert in traditional Chinese medicine, summarized the achievements in Chinese acupuncture and moxibustion prior to the Wei and Jin dynasties. It is the earliest Chinese book extant on the subject.

6-6-3

6-6-1

6-6-2

6-6-4 Model of a tipper The model was made by the National Museum of Chinese History on the basis of the *History of the Three Kingdoms* and a modern hand-driven tipper used in the Luoyang area.

6-6-4

6-6-5 Rubbing of a fragment of the stone classics engraved in three kinds of script Relic of Wei of the Three Kingdoms Period, fragment 112 cm high, 46 cm wide; unearthed in 1922 in Luoyang, Henan Province. In the third century, during the Zhengshi reign of Wei, parts of two Confucian classics, *Book of History* and *Spring and Autumn Annals*, were engraved on stone tablets in three scripts – great seal script, small seal script and official script. These different scripts reflect the evolution of the style of writing in ancient China.

6-6-6 Lü's brick, made in the fourth year of the Xianning reign Western Jin, length 34.8 cm, width 17.2 cm, thickness 5.8 cm; unearthed in 1918 at Fengtai County, Anhui Province. Xianning was the reign title of Sima Yan, the first emperor of Jin; the fourth year of his reign was AD 278.

6-6-5

6-6-6

6-6-6*

6-6-7

6-6-8

6-6-7 Ladies on an excursion (brick engraving) Southern Dynasties, length 38 cm, width 19 cm, thickness 6.3 cm; unearthed in 1958 in Deng County, Henan Province.

6-6-8 Phoenix (brick engraving) Southern Dynasties, length 38.7 cm, width 18.9 cm, thickness 6.3 cm; unearthed in 1958 in Deng County, Henan Province.

6-6-9 Arched stone door of Yonggu Mausoleum Northern Wei, lintel 224 cm long, 50 cm wide, 19 cm thick; frame 168 cm long, 22 cm wide, 22 cm thick; stone block under door 30 cm high, 41 cm wide, 45 cm long. Yonggu Mausoleum, situated at the southern foot of Mount Liang (ancient name Mount Fang) to the north of present-day Datong, Shanxi Province, is the tomb of Empress Wenming, née Feng, wife of the Northern Wei emperor Wencheng (born Tuoba Jun).

6-6-9*

6-6-9

6-6-10 Black glazed pottery *hunping* with pavilion and Buddhist statuettes Relic of Wu of the Three Kingdoms, height 42 cm, belly diameter 26 cm, base diameter 16.3 cm; unearthed in Nanjing, Jiangsu Province. *Hunping* was a uniquely shaped funerary object.

6-6-11

6-6-11*

6-6-10

6-6-11 Taoist images sculpted with Wang Ashan's fund Northern Wei, height 27.8 cm. Wang Ashan, who provided the money for the sculpture, was a woman Taoist. The sculpture was made in 527, the first year of the Longxu reign of Xiao Baoyin, sixth son of Emperor Min of Qi of the Southern Dynasties.

Sui, Tang and Five Dynasties (581—960)

Sui Unifies the North and South

In 581 Yang Jian, a noble of the Northern Zhou, seized political power and established the Sui Dynasty. In 589 he conquered Chen, the last of the Southern Dynasties, and unified the country, putting an end to the 270 years of division between north and south. Unification of the country by the Sui laid the foundation for the prosperity of the Tang Dynasty.

After establishing the Sui Dynasty, Yang Jian set up a government at the central level consisting of three councils and six ministries. In local administration, he adopted a two-level system of prefectures and counties. The appointment or dismissal of all local officials was made by the central government, and an imperial examination system for prospective officials was instituted. Corvée labor and taxation were reduced and production in all fields was encouraged, resulting in a rapid development of agri-culture, handicrafts and commerce. Two important construction projects were completed – the Grand Canal linking north and south and the Zhaozhou Bridge, the oldest spandrel stone arch bridge in the world.

Along with the development of the country's economy and the increase in its social wealth, the ruling clique became increasingly corrupt, especially during the reign of the second Sui emperor Yangdi. On the one hand, the government carried out lavish construction projects; on the other, the emperor repeatedly went on pleasure trips, and wantonly engaged in military ventures. Ultimately, this led to peasant uprisings that toppled the dynasty in less than 40 years.

7-1-1

7-1-1 Pottery figurine of a woman rider Sui funerary object, overall height 37.5 cm; unearthed in 1956 at Guizishan, Wuhan, Hubei Povince.

7-1-2 Pottery figurine of a civil official Sui funerary object, 65 cm tall; unearthed in 1956 from a Sui tomb at Zhoujia Dawan, Wuhan, Hubei Province.

7-1-3 Celadon flask with four rings, hornless dragon handle and chicken-head spout Sui water container, height 25 cm, mouth diameter 6.6 cm, base diameter 7 cm; unearthed in 1956 from Sui Tomb No.241 in Wuhan, Hubei Province.

7-1-3

7-1-2

7-1-4

7-1-5

7-1-4 Stone coffin and other relics from Li Jingxun's tomb Sui Dynasty, length 192 cm, width 89 cm, height 122 cm; unearthed in 1957 from the tomb of Li Jingxun, a young noblewoman, in Xi'an, Shaanxi Province. The exquisitely made relics in the coffin reflect the high level of architecture, science and technology, handicrafts, painting and sculpture of the Sui. The stone coffin shown here is a replica.

7-1-5 White porcelain flask with twin body and dragon handles Sui Dynasty, height 18.6 cm, mouth diameter 4.5 cm, belly diameter 6.3 cm; unearthed in 1957 from Li Jingxun's tomb, Xi'an, Shaanxi Province.

7-1-6 Gold headdress with flower-and-butterfly design, inlaid with pearls and precious stones Sui Dynasty, length 11.47 cm, width 8.3 cm; unearthed in 1957 from Li Jingxun tomb, Xi'an, Shaanxi Province.

7-1-6

7-1-6*

7-1-7 Map of the Grand Canal, Sui Dynasty The Grand Canal, running from Yuhang (now Hangzhou, Zhejiang Province) in the south, to Zuo Prefecture (now Beijing) in the north, is a great man-made waterway with a total length of more than 2,000 kilometers. It has played an important role in strengthening economic and cultural intercourse between north and south and promoting the development of the country's economy.

7-1-8 Stone slab on balustrade of Zhaozhou Bridge Sui Dynasty, 212 cm long, 84.5 cm high; unearthed in 1952 at the site of Anji Bridge in Zhao County, Hebei Province. Zhaozhou Bridge, also known as Anji Bridge, is 50.82 cm long and 9.6 cm wide; the span of its stone arch is 37.37 meters. On the left and right exterior curves of the stone arch are two pairs of smaller arches (spandrels). These reduce the overall weight of the bridge and economize on the use of stone. They also divert part of the flow during high water season. The bridge has withstood floods, quakes, the weight of heavy vehicles and inclemencies of wind and rain for over 1,300 years.

隋运河图

图例
⊕ 都 城
○ 其它居民点
⊕ 粮 仓
— 运 河

7-1-7

7-1-8

隋 运 河 图

7-1-8*

7-2-1

The Prime Tang

In 618 Li Yuan, an aristocrat of the Sui Dynasty, established the Tang Dynasty. Chang'an (now Xi'an, Shaanxi Province) and Luoyang were the two capitals of the dynasty. Chang'an, the western capital, was not only the nation's political, economic and cultural center but also the world's largest metropolis during the Middle Ages. It had a perimeter of 35 kilometers and a population of one million, including several thousand merchants and students from other countries. Luoyang, the eastern capital, was a hub of transportation through which all grains and supplies transported by water to the western capital had to pass. Hanjia Granary was a large government storage in Luoyang, occupying an area of 400,000 square meters. It contained several hundred pits, which could store several million kilos of grain.

In the early Tang, the country was strong and prosperous and the government honest and clean. Taxes and corvée were reduced, and the feudal economy and culture flourished. It was a period known as the "Zhenguan era of good government" and "Kaiyuan era of good government," during which China stood in the forefront among the world's civilized countries. It lasted until 755 when a rebellion led by An Lushan and Shi Siming broke out and the fortunes of the dynasty declined.

7-2-1 Portrait of Tang Emperor Taizong
Li Shiming (599-649), or Emperor Taizong, was the second emperor of the Tang Dynasty. He was an outstanding politician and strategist. During his reign, a period known in history as the "Zhenguan era of good government" appeared.

7-2-2 Painted gilded pottery figurine of a civil official Tang funerary object, 1st year (AD 664) of the Lingde reign, height 69 cm; unearthed in 1972 from the tomb of Zheng Rentai in Liquan County, Shaanxi Province.

7-2-3 Painted gilded pottery figurine of a warrior Tang funerary object, 1st year (AD 664) of the Lingde reign, height 71.5 cm; unearthed in 1972 from the tomb of Zheng Rentai in Liquan County, Shaanxi Province.

7-2-2   7-2-3

7-2-4

7-2-5

7-2-5*

7-2-4 Iron sluice gate in Chang'an City's sewerage Tang Dynasty, 72.4 cm high, 65.6 cm wide, 4 cm thick; unearthed in 1954 in the Western Inner Garden of Chang'an City, Xi'an, Shaanxi Province.

7-2-5 Musicians on camelback, three-color figurines Tang funerary object, 11th year (AD 723) of the Kaiyuan reign, height to the top of the camel's head 58.4 cm, length 43.4 cm; unearthed in 1957 from the tomb of Xianyu Tinghui in Xi'an, Shaanxi Province.

7-2-6 Grain stored in Pit 160 of the Hanjia

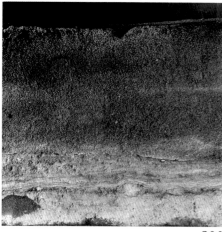

7-2-6

Granary and the structure of the pit's bottom Tang Dynasty, length 52.2 cm, width 33 cm, height 47 cm; unearthed in 1971 at the site of the Hanjia Granary, Luoyang, Henan Province.

7-2-7 Black glazed three-color terra-cotta horse figurine Tang Dynasty, height 67.2 cm, length 78.2 cm; unearthed in 1972 at Guanlin, Luoyang, Henan Province.

7-2-7

7-2-7*

Ethnic Tribes on the Borders of the Tang Empire

Along with the unification of the country and the development of its economy, the Tang Dynasty expanded and strengthened its relations with ethnic minorites along the borders by setting up regional administrations, encouraging intermarriage, forming alliances, conferring titles and carrying out business transactions, chiefly in tea and horses. Many minority nationals were given official posts at the Tang court or became officers in the Tang army. Regional administrations were set up in places inhabited by the Turks and Uygurs in the north and northwest, at Tubo in the west, at Nanzhao in the southwest and at Bohai in the northeast. The minorities assimilated the advanced economy and culture of the Han in the course of their development and in turn influenced and enriched Han culture, thus strengthening the political, economic and cultural ties between the Hans and minorities and promoting the development of the border areas.

7-3-1

7-3-3 **Glazed beast-head** Structural part of a Tang building, remnant height 26.5 cm; unearthed from the ruins of Longquanfu, Upper Capital of Bohai, Ning'an County, Heilongjiang Province. The relic shows the influence of Tang culture on the Bohai people.

7-3-3

7-3-1 Dumplings and other delicacies
Tang Dynasty, unearthed in 1972 in Turpan, Xinjiang Uygur Autonomous Region. The discovery shows the mutual influence on lifestyles between Xinjiang and wthe interior.
7-3-2 Tang emperor seated in a sedan chair, receiving an envoy (printed copy) Tang Dynasty painting by Yan Liben, 38.5 x 129.6 cm. The painting depicts Emperor Taizong seated in an imperial sedan chair, receiving a Tubo envoy sent by Songtsan Gambo to propose a marriage. Tang princess Wencheng's marriage to Songtsan Gambo helped promote the economic and cultural exchange between the Hans and Tibetans. The original painting is in the Palace Museum.

7-3-2

Economy of the Tang Dynasty

There was a long period of national unity, social stability and fairly rapid development of productive forces during the Tang Dynasty, whose feudal economy saw great progress.

New farm tools such as crankshaft sickles and wheels with tubes rotated by water power or oxen appeared, and the government attached great importance to the construction of water conservancy projects. Improvements in farm tools and development of water conservation helped to expand the acreage of cultivated and irrgated land and raised the output of both grain and cash crops. In the handicrafts, notable improvements in production techniques and in the mechanism governing division of labor were made in both government and private sectors. New techniques were invented in ceramics, such as splash-glaze, twisted-paste glaze, underglaze painting and three-color glaze, so that diverse decorations became a special feature of Tang pottery and porcelain. In silk weaving, weft patterns gradually replaced the traditional warp patterns and the wide use of such techniques as tie-and-dye, wax-resist dyeing and sandwich-dyeing made Tang silk fabrics more colorful. Exquisitely made gold and silver articles and finely cast bronze mirrors are also examples of the development of handicrafts in the Tang Dynasty.

Transportation progressed and commerce prospered, especially after the mid-Tang when there appeared the night market, the "counting house" dealing in deposits and cashing, *fei qian* which is similar to the money order, and trade associations known as guilds. All these laid the foundation for the highly prosperous economy of the Song Dynasty, the next major dynasty in Chinese history.

7-4-1

7-4-1 Wheel with bamboo tubes (model) Reproduced by the National Museum of Chinese History based on Chen Tingzhang's *Rhyme Prose on Water Wheels* and Wang Zhen's *Argricultural Treatise*. The wheel is driven by water power. The tubes discharge water when they are rotated to a high position and are refilled when lowered.

7-4-2 Brocade with rings of pearl in deer design Tang Dynasty, length 19.5 cm, width 16.5 cm; unearthed in 1966 in Turpan, Xinjiang Uygur Autonomous Region.

7-4-2

7-4-3

7-4-3*

7-4-3 Silver plate with gilded lion design
Tang Dynasty, length 6.7 cm, diameter 40 cm;
unearthed in 1956 in Xi'an, Shaanxi Province.
**7-4-4 Bronze mirror with shell-inlaid design
of flowers, birds and figures**   Tang Dynasty,
diameter 23.9 cm; unearthed in 1955 from a
Tang tomb in Luoyang, Henan Province. The
design was made by sticking thin pieces of
shells with lacquer onto the back of the
mirror.

7-4-4

7-4-4*

7-4-5

7-4-5 "Secret color" porcelain plate with sunflower-petal design Tang Dynasty, diameter 35 cm; unearthed in 1989 at Digong, Famen Temple, Fufeng County, Shanxi Province. The name "secret color" appeared on a list of clothes and other articles unearthed at the same time, showing that it was a product of the Yue Kiln made for use in the imperial palace.

7-4-6 White porcelain lamp with lotus-petal design Tang Dynasty, height 30.5 cm; unearthed in 1956 from a Tang tomb at Liujiaqu, Shaan County, Henan Province.

7-4-6

7-4-7*

7-4-7 Bluish yellow glazed porcelain plate with orchid design Tang Dynasty, height 4.1 cm, mouth diameter 15.5 cm; unearthed in 1978 at the site of the Tongguan Kiln in Changsha, Hunan Province.

7-4-8 Splash-glazed porcelain ewer Tang Dynasty, height 30.9 cm, base diameter 9.1 cm; unearthed in 1978 at the site of the Tongguan Kiln in Changsha, Hunan Province. Splash-glazed porcelain was made by splashing different tinges of glaze on the base glaze. It was the forerunner of the technique of furnace transmutation (underglaze blue turned red) of the Jun Kiln of the Song Dynasty.

7-4-7

7-4-9 Porcelain pillow made with two-color twisted clay Tang Dynasty, height 7.7 cm, length 14.7 cm, width 10 cm; unearthed in 1956 from a Tang tomb at Liujiaqu, Shaan County, Henan Province.

7-4-10 *Kaiyuan Tongbao* coin Tang Dynasty, diameter 2.4 cm, weight 4 grams.

7-4-8

7-4-9

7-4-10

Economic and Cultural Relations with Foreign Countries

During the Tang Dynasty, the doors of China were opened wider than ever before, and contacts with foreign countries were all the more frequent. Through the busy Silk Road that started from the Tang capital Chang'an (today's Xi'an, Shaanxi Province) in the east, passed through the heartlands of Asia and terminated at Constantinople (now Istanbul, Turkey), capital of the Eastern Roman Empire, the Tang empire exported silk, porcelain wares and other commodities to the West. And along the same route, jewels, medicinal herbs, and perfumes from the West were introduced into China. Thus the influence of Chinese culture spread far and wide. After the mid-Tang, with the progress made in shipbuilding and navigation technology, maritime trade routes developed, too, the importance of which increased with each passing day. Along the Silk Roads by land and sea, trade caravans, travelers and students came and went in an endless stream. Many foreign merchants settled down in China while Chinese artisans traveled far to the Arabian peninsula to engage in handicraft production.

Many Chinese eminent monks went abroad to study Buddhist doctrines or give lectures. Among them the most famous were Xuanzang, who went west to India to seek Buddhist scriptures, and Jianzhen, who went east to Japan to give lectures. Both made great contributions to economic and cultural exchanges between China and foreign countries.

7-5-2

7-5-1 Sketch map of the Silk Road in the Tang Dynasty

7-5-2 Printed silk gauze with hunting design in dark green Tang Dynasty, length 35 cm, width 18 cm; unearthed in 1968 in Turpan, Xinjiang Uygur Autonomous Region.

7-5-3 Pottery figurine of a traveler from Tajik Tang funerary object, height 27 cm.

唐代"丝绸之路"示意图

图 例

☐   都城
○   其他居民点
师子国 故国名
卡拉奇 今注记
——   陆上路线
——   海上路线
-----   河运路线

7-5-1

7-5-3

佛　敕　法　二　大
像　造　師　年　唐
供　釋　立　三　龍
養　迦　奘　藏　朔

7-5-4*

7-5-4

7-5-5

7-5-6 **Three-color glazed pottery figurine of a camel and rider** Tang relic, 11th year (AD 723) of the Kaiyuan reign, overall height 40.2 cm, length 48 cm; unearthed in 1957 from the tomb of Xianyu Tinghui in Xi'an, Shaanxi Province.

7-5-6*

7-5-5*

7-5-4 **Stone seat of the Buddha inscribed with the name of Xuanzang** Tang relic, 2nd year (AD 662) of the Longshuo reign, height 36 cm, diameter of upper part 49.5 cm; unearthed in 1977 at the ruins of Yuhua Palace, Tongchuan, Shaanxi Province. Xuanzang was the author of the book *Records of the Western Regions During the Tang Dynasty*, in which he described what he saw and heard on his trips to 138 countries and regions between 627-645. The stone seat is a relic left by him during his stay at the Yuhua Temple.

7-5-5 **Ivory sculpture of a bodhisattva riding an elephant** Buddhist sculpture of the 7th century in Yulin Cave, Anxi County, Gansu Province, height 15.8 cm, thickness 7.5 cm; said to have been brought to China from India. The sculpture can be opened and closed. When closed, it is the image of a bodhisattva riding an elephant and holding a pagoda. When opened, each side consists of 25 squares, on which are carvings of the Jataka story about Sakyamuni's earlier incarnations.

7-5-6

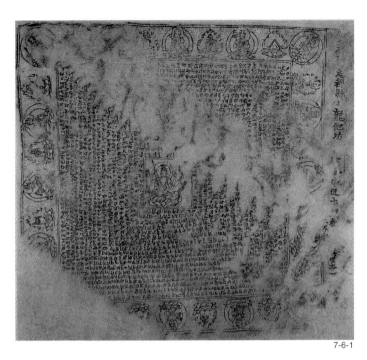

7-6-1

Science, Culture and Social Life in the Tang Dynasty

The Tang empire's extensive and frequent contacts with foreign countries produced a culture that was grandiose and diverse in nature. It had a profound influence not only on later generations but also on world culture. In the field of science and technology, major breakthroughs and innovations were made in astronomy, geography, medical and pharmaceutical science, as well as block printing. In literature and art, especially in poetry, calligraphy, painting, sculpture, music and dance, great achievements were made and eminent artisans and men of letters emerged in large numbers. Cities thrived and social life became richer and more colorful. Changes in the lifestyle of the Tang people and their social custom are reflected in their costumes, recreation and articles of daily use.

7-6-1 Buddhist Dharani Charm, block printed by Bianjia of Longchifang, Chengdu County, Chengdu Prefecture Tang Dynasty, length 30.5 cm, width 34.3 cm; unearthed in 1944 from a Tang tomb at Wangjianglou, Chengdu, Sichuan Province.

7-6-2 Sketch map showing Monk Yixing's survey of the meridian Tang Dynasty, 12th year (AD 724) of the Kaiyuan reign, Monk Yixing directed a survey in the Henan area to measure the length of the sun's shadow and the altitude of the North Pole. This is the first recorded ground measurement of the meridian line.

7-6-3 *A New Compendium of Materia Medica* A facsimile edition made in Japan; the original book was compiled and written by Sun Jing and others of the Tang Dynasty. Made public in 659, the fourth year of the Xianqing reign of Tang, it was the first government-authorized pharmacopoeia in China. The section "Drug Illustrations" is the earliest illustrated list of Chinese medicinal drugs.

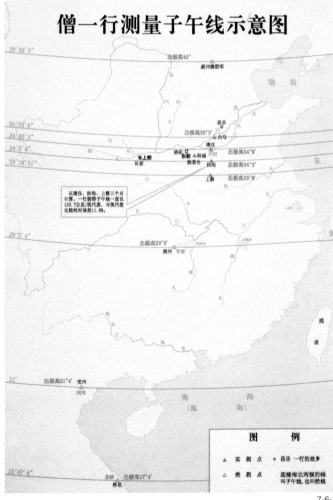

7-6-2

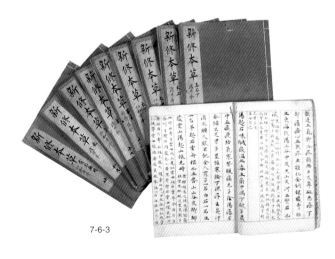

7-6-3

7-6-4 Three-color sitting female figurine
Tang funerary object, height 28.2 cm;
unearthed in 1955 at Baijiakou in Xi'an,
Shaanxi Province. The garment, skirt, and silk
cape worn by the figurine were fashions of
the Tang Dynasty. The way she sits shows
that the habits of people of the Tang era had
changed; instead of sitting on the ground,
they now sat on stools with feet dangling.

**7-6-5 Stone carved warrior figurine traced in
gold** Tang funerary object, 28th year (AD
740) of the Kaiyuan reign, 40.5 cm tall;
unearthed in 1958 from the tomb of Yang Sixu
in Xi'an, Shaanxi Province. The warrior's
clothes, though in an exotic style, represent
the most popular men's fashion of the time.

**7-6-6 Pottery figurines of the twelve zodiac
animals** Tang Dynasty, height 36.5-42.5 cm;
unearthed in 1955 at Hansen Village, Xi'an,
Shaanxi Province. In ancient China, the Ten
Heavenly Stems and Twelve Earthly Branches
were used to designate years, months, days
and hours. Later, twelve animals were
matched with the Earthly Branches, and were
called "the twelve animals symbolic of years
of birth."

7-6-4

7-6-5

7-6-6

7-6-7

7-6-7 Pottery figurines of musicians accompanying a dance Tang funerary objects, 11-11.5 cm tall; unearthed in 1955 from a Tang tomb in Xi'an, Shaanxi Province.
7-6-8 Mural of a dancing girl in red Tang Dynasty, 3rd year (AD 658) of the Xianqing reign, decorative picture from a Tang tomb chamber, 115.5 cm high, 69.5 cm wide; unearthed in 1957 from a Tang tomb at Guodu Township, Xi'an, Shaanxi Province.

7-6-8

7-6-9

7-6-10

7-6-9 Painted pottery polo players Tang funerary objects, height 32-36 cm; unearthed in 1958 from a Tang tomb in Xi'an, Shaanxi Province. Polo was a popular game in the Tang Dynasty.

7-6-10 White-glazed porcelain tea vase Tang Dynasty, height 16.7 cm, mouth diameter 9.6 cm, base diameter 7.1 cm; unearthed in 1956 at Liujiaqu, Shaan County, Henan Province. Water was boiled in the vase, then poured over tea leaves in a cup. The use of such vases marked the beginning of steeping tea in boiling water.

7-6-11 Hall in Foguang Temple (model) The temple is located at Dou Village, Wutai County, Shanxi Province. Built in 857, 11th year of the Dazhong reign of Tang, the hall is one of the earliest wooden structures extant in China. It still houses clay sculptures and murals of the Tang Dynasty.

7-6-11

Peasant Uprising in the Late Tang Dynasty and the Period of the Five Dynasties and Ten Kingdoms

Arrogation of all powers by eunuchs, setting up of separatist regimes by military governors, intensified annexation of land and excessive taxes led to a large-scale peasant uprising led by Huang Chao during the late Tang.

Eventually, in 907, the Tang Dynasty collapsed and Zhu Wen, a former high official, proclaimed himself emperor of a new dynasty, which was known in history as the Later Liang. During the next 50-odd years, from 907 to 960, the Yellow River valley came under the rule of five successive short-lived dynasties: the Later Liang, Later Tang, Later Jin, Later Han and Later Zhou, collectively called the Five Dynasties. At the same time, south China and Shanxi were ruled by ten separatist regimes, sometimes superseding each other, often coexisting: the Early Shu, Wu, Min, Wuyue, Chu, Southern Han, Nanping, Later Shu, Southern Tang and Northern Han, known in history as the Ten Kingdoms. Dur-

7-7-1

7-7-1*

ing this period, the north was plagued with wars and political unrest, but the south was relatively stable with a fairly well developed society and economy. Towards the end of the Five Dynasties, the Later Zhou introduced a series of political and economic reforms that had a positive effect on social stability and economic recovery. This paved the way for the reunification of the country under the Song.

7-7-2

7-7-1 Iron pledge for Qian Liu Relic of Tang, 4th year (AD 897) of the Qianning reign, 45 cm long, 29 cm wide, 0.3 cm thick. Under the pressure of peasant uprisings, and in order to win over local military governors, Emperor Zhaozong of Tang bestowed upon Qian Liu, who later founded the kingdom of Wuyue in 907, an iron pledge that exempted him from the death penalty even if he committed capital offences.

7-7-2 Painted pottery figurine of a civil official Funerary object of Min, one of the Ten Kingdoms, height 62.2 cm; unearthed in 1965 from the tomb of Liu Hua in the northern suburbs of Fuzhou, Fujian Province.

7-7-4

7-7-3

7-7-5 Gilded brass knocker Relic of Early Shu, one of the Ten Kingdoms; overall height 37.8 cm, diameter 29.4 cm; unearthed from the tomb of Wang Jian, Chengdu, Sichuan Province.

7-7-6 Celadon jar with six loop handles Five Dynasties, height 19.5 cm; unearthed in 1954 at Shima Village, Panyu County, Guangdong Province.

7-7-3 Peacock blue glazed pottery vase with three loop handles Relic of Min, one of the Ten Kingdoms, height 75 cm, mouth diameter 17 cm, base diameter 16 cm; unearthed in 1965 from the tomb of Liu Hua in the northern suburbs of Fuzhou, Fujian Province. A Persian pottery vase, it is evidence of the cultural exchange between China and other countries in those days.

7-7-4 Gilded bronze statue of Goddess of Mercy Five Dynasties, overall height 38.5 cm, base width 20 cm, height of halo 39.9 cm; unearthed in 1958 at the Ten-Thousand Buddha Pagoda in Jinhua County, Zhejiang Province.

7-7-5

7-7-6

Song, Liao, Western Xia, Jin and Yuan (960—1368)

Founded in 960, the Song Dynasty lasted a total of 320 years, from the 60s of the 10th century to the 70s of the 13th century. It was an important period in China's feudal society, one that carried on past traditions and opened new vistas for the future. The dynasty had its capital at Kaifeng in the Central Plains in the beginning, but moved south to Hangzhou in 1127. Historians call the earlier and later periods of the dynasty with different capitals the Northern Song and Southern Song. The Song empire was composed mainly of Han Chinese. A number of minority regimes existed along its border for a long time. They included the Liao founded by the Qidan people, the Western Xia founded by the Dangxiang, and the Jin founded by the Nuzhen. These regimes waged wars on the Song, but there was also a relatively long period of peaceful coexistence.

In the 70s of the 13th century, the Mongolians founded the Yuan Dynasty and unified China, ending an era of many coexisting regimes that had lasted more than 370 years, from the Five Dynasties through the Southern Song.

Simultaneous Existence of the Song, Liao, Western Xia and Jin

In 960, Zhao Kuangyin, a high-ranking military leader of the Later Zhou, staged a mutiny and founded the Song Dynasty with its capital at Kaifeng. It is known in history as the Northern Song. The Song government eliminated the separatist regimes Later Shu, Southern Han, Southern Tang and Northern Han, unifying a vast area from Guangdong and Guangxi in the far south to the Yellow River valley.

There were also several minority ethnic regimes that existed side by side with the Northern Song: Liao in the northeast, Western Xia in the northwest, and Tubo and Dali in the southwest. The Song waged wars on the Liao and Western Xia, but eventually they concluded a peace agreement and co-existed peacefully for some time. In 1115 Akutta, chief of the Nuzhen tribe, established the Jin Dynasty, making Huining Prefecture (now Acheng County, Heilongjiang Province) his capital. Between 1125 and 1127 he conquered both the Liao and the Northern Song, and occupied the vast area north of the Huai River.

After the fall of the Northern Song Dynasty, Zhao Gou, the ninth son of Song Emperor Huizong, established the Southern Song in Nanjing (today's Shangqiu, Henan Province). Later he moved his capital to Lin'an (today's Hangzhou, Zhejiang Province). During the early years of the Southern Song Dynasty, the Jin frequently invaded the south but met with stubborn resistance from the Song army and people. Song general Yue Fei led his army in a northern expedition that recovered some lost territory. In 1141, the Song and Jin signed the Shaoxing Peace Agreement, ending their military conflicts but ushering in a long period of political confrontation.

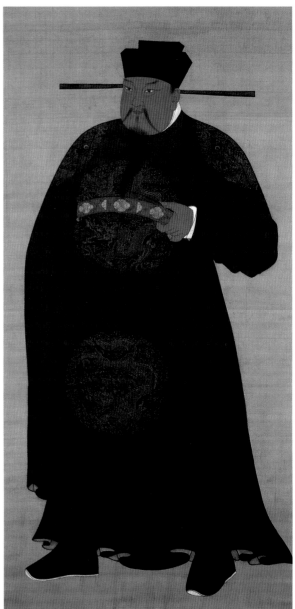

8-1-1 Portrait of Zhao Kuangyin Painted by a Ming Dynasty artist. Zhao Kuangyin (927-976), Emperor Taizu, was the founder of the Northern Song Dynasty. During the 17 years of his reign, the centralized state power of the feudal autocracy was further strengthened.

北宋东京城图

8-1-2

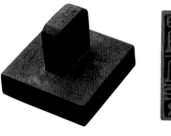 

8-1-4

8-1-2 Map of the Eastern Capital of the Northern Song Kaifeng Prefecture (now Kaifeng, Henan Province) was the capital of the country during the Northern Song. Called the Eastern Capital, it consisted of an outer city, an inner city and an imperial city. Because of repeated flooding of the Yellow River, most parts of the city proper are buried under modern Kaifeng. The map is based on archaeological finds.

8-1-3 Brick from an iron pagoda with unicorn design Song Dynasty, length 35.5 cm, width 20 cm, thickness 6.8 cm.

8-1-4 Copper seal of the "5th Du under the 2nd Command, 4th Army, of the Left Imperial Guards" Northern Song, length 5.5 cm, width 5.3 cm, height 4.2 cm. Du was the basic unit of the imperial guards.

8-1-3

8-1-5

8-1-5*

8-1-5 Copper weight of the Jiayou reign
Measure of Northern Song Dynasty, 30 cm high, 20 cm thick, 64 kilograms in weight; unearthed in 1975 in Xiangtan, Hunan Province. It was a standard measure issued by the Song government. There are inscriptions on the front and back. The inscription on the front says, "Cast in the first year (AD 1056) of the Jiayou reign"; the one on the back says, "Weight of copper norm 100 catties." Calculated on the basis of the actual weight of the norm, one catty in those days was equal to 640 grams.

8-1-6 "Illustration of Imperial Guard of Honor" (section) Northern Song, overall length 51.4 cm, width 1481 cm. The illustration depicts a grandiose scene of a Song emperor going to the south of Kaifeng to offer sacrifices to heaven and earth.

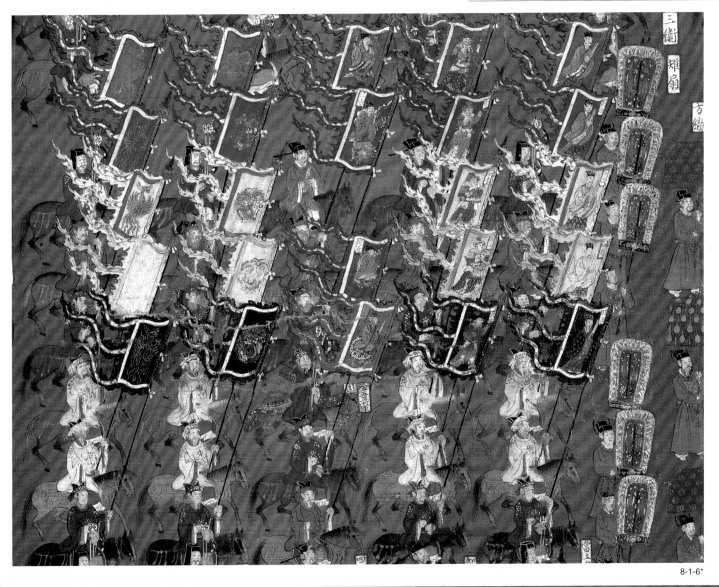

8-1-6*

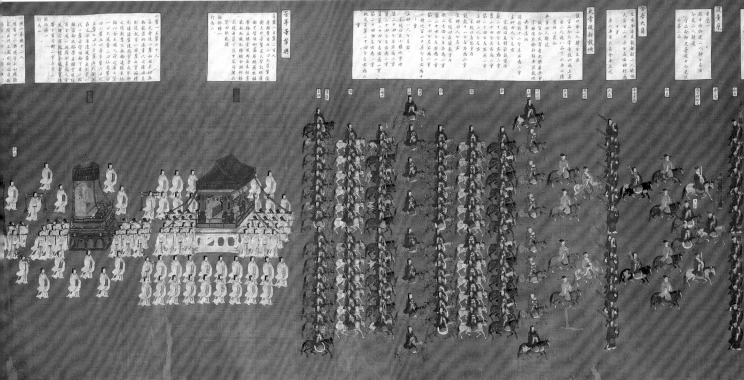

8-1-6

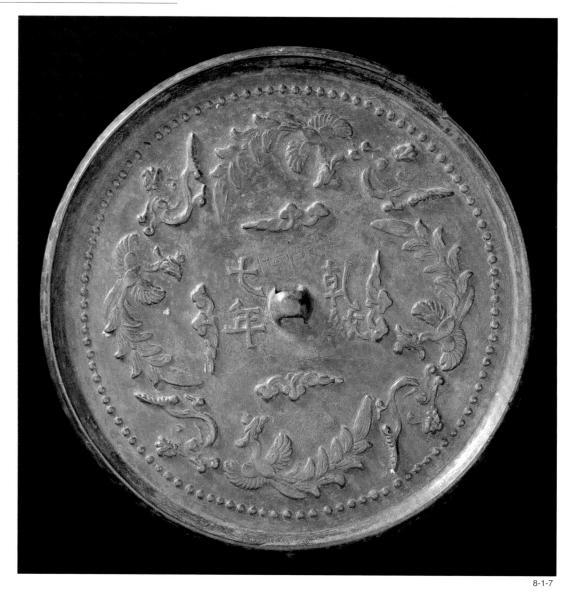

8-1-7

8-1-8

8-1-7 Bronze mirror cast in the 7th year of the Qiantong reign   Liao, diameter 19 cm, thickness 0.7 cm, weight 650 grams.

8-1-8 Brown glazed porcelain stirrup-shaped pot   Liao, height 24 cm; unearthed in 1956 at Fuxing Gate, Beijing.

8-1-9 Cockscomb-shaped silver pot with gilded deer design   Liao, height 26.3 cm, mouth diameter 5.5 cm, base length 21.1 cm; unearthed in 1979 in Chifeng, Inner Mongolia Autonomous Region.

8-1-10 Three-color glazed plate shaped like a begonia, with impressed fish design   Liao, 2.1 cm high, 27.6 cm long; unearthed in 1959 from a Liao tomb in Ningcheng County, Inner Mongolia Autonomous Region.

8-1-9

8-1-10

8-1-11

8-1-13

8-1-12

8-1-11 Copper plate with an edict, "Urgent, go swiftly on horseback"   Western Xia, overall height 18.5 cm, diameter 14.7 cm.

8-1-12 Ridge-end used in an imperial mausoleum   Western Xia, height 152 cm, width 92 cm, thickness 32 cm; unearthed in 1972 from an imperial mausoleum of the Western Xia in Yinchuan, Ningxia Hui Autonomous Region.

8-1-13 Brown glazed porcelain flask with carved design   Western Xia, height 33.3 cm, mouth diameter 9 cm, belly diameter 32 cm; obtained in 1985 from Haiyuan County, Ningxia Hui Autonomous Region.

8-1-14

8-1-15

8-1-14 Big bronze mirror with twin-fish design Jin, diameter 36.7 cm, weight 4300 grams; unearthed in 1964 from Acheng County, Heilongjiang Province.

8-1-15 Casket with pendants Jin, full length 32 cm; unearthed in 1973 from a Jin tomb in Suibin County, Heilongjiang Province. It was a waist pendant used by aristocrats of the Nuzhen tribe.

8-1-16 Picture of four Song generals Southern Song, 26 x 90.6 cm; said to have been painted by Liu Songnian. The four generals shown in the picture are Liu Guangshi, Han Shizhong, Zhang Jun and Yue Fei, all famous for their resistance against the Jin in the early years of the Southern Song.

8-1-16

Economy of the Song Dynasty

During the Northern and Southern Song dynasties, the focal point of the country's economy was moved to the south. In a relatively stable situation, notable progress was made in the social economy. The area of cultivated land was expanded, grain output increased steadily, and paddy-rice planting was extended to the north.

In the handicraft industry, there was a broader scope of business for handicraft workshops, greater commercialization of household handicrafts, and increased specialization. In mining,

8-2-1

metallurgy, shipbuilding, paper making, printing, ceramics, and spinning and weaving, the Song Dynasty surpassed all previous dynasties in terms of both technology and output. Song porcelain, in particular, was far superior to the products of previous periods in quality, glaze color and pattern, and in production scale and exports. Porcelain wares made in the five famous kilns of the time — the Jun Kiln, Ru Kiln, Ge Kiln, Guan Kiln and Ding Kiln — enjoyed high reputation both at home and abroad. Large and medium-sized cities emerged rapidly, village markets were set up all over the countryside, and mercantile economy developed as never before. Foreign trade flourished at an unprecedented speed, with Guangzhou, Quanzhou and Minzhou (now Ningbo, Zhejiang Province) as the leading ports for overseas trade. The government set up a custom-function office to manage the export and import business. Chinese goods were exported to the Korean Peninsula and Japan in the east, and to Western Asia and Africa in the west.

8-2-1 Iron hoe Northern Song, 63.7 cm long, blade 22.1 cm wide; unearthed in 1952 at Baisha Reservoir, Yu County, Henan Province.

8-2-2 Two-ear vase Product of the Guan Kiln, Southern Song, height 22.8 cm, mouth diameter 8.3 cm, base diameter 9.6 cm.

8-2-3 Burner with fish-shaped handles Product of the Ge Kiln, Song Dynasty, height 8.8 cm, mouth diameter 11.9 cm, base diameter 9.2 cm.

8-2-4 Basin Product of the Ru Kiln, Northern Song, height 5 cm, mouth diameter 16.4 cm, base diameter 13.2 cm.

8-2-2

8-2-3

8-2-4

8-2-4*

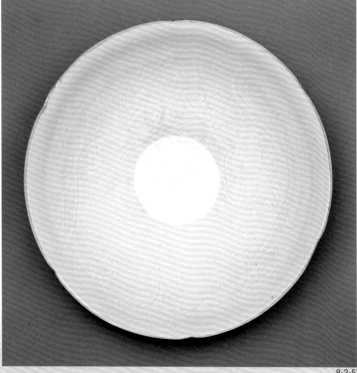

8-2-5*

8-2-5

8-2-5 Mallow-petal bowl with incised day lily design   Product of the Ding Kiln, Northern Song, height 6.1 cm, mouth diameter 21.4 cm, base diameter 6.6 cm.

8-2-6 Begonia-shaped rose red flowerpot   Product of the Jun Kiln, Song Dynasty, height 14.5 cm, mouth diameter 19.5-24.5 cm.

8-2-6

8-2-7 Lacquered toilet case Song Dynasty, height 17.3 cm, diameter 16.4 cm; small box height 3.6 cm, diameter 5.5 cm.

8-2-8 Sunflower-shaped mirror from Jizhou Southern Song, diameter 17.4 cm, thickness 0.4 cm.

8-2-9 Copper plate for printing paper money called *huizi* Southern Song, 18.4 x 12.4 cm.

8-2-7

8-2-8

8-2-9

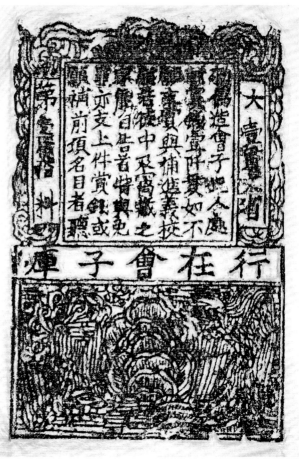

8-2-9*

8-2-10

8-2-11

8-2-12

8-2-10 Copper plate for printing advertisements of the Liu Family Needle Shop Song Dynasty, length 12.4 cm, width 13.2 cm.

8-2-11 Woman Cleaning Fish (brick engraving) Song Dynasty, length 34.2 cm, width 24 cm.

8-2-12 Bronze mirror decorated with a marine ship Song Dynasty, diameter 17.3 cm, thickness 0.6 cm.

Science and Culture of the Song Dynasty

Notable achievements were made in science and culture during the Song Dynasty. New discoveries and inventions were recorded in astronomy, mathematics, mechanics, medicine and pharmacology, gun powder, the compass, type printing, and ship-building. In some areas, China was far ahead of the rest of the world and made great contributions to the advancement of world science and technology. Chinese literature, history, philosophy and arts also reached new heights. A number of eminent scientists, inventors, historians, philosophers, men of letters, painters and poets emerged, and many famous works of the period are gems in the treasure house of world culture.

8-3-1 Rubbing from a stone portrait of Su Shi Su Shi (1037-1101), styled "Retired Scholar Dongpo", was a celebrated man of letters of the Northern Song. The original stone portrait is in the Six-Banyan Pagoda in Guangzhou, Guangdong Province.

8-3-2 Portrait of Sima Guang Sima Guang (1019-1086) was a noted politician and historian of the Northern Song.

8-3-1

8-3-2

8-3-3 Baiyi inkslab Northern Song, length 18 cm, width 10.5 cm, thickness 5 cm.

8-3-3*

8-3-3

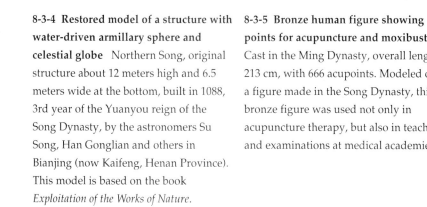

8-3-4 **Restored model of a structure with water-driven armillary sphere and celestial globe** Northern Song, original structure about 12 meters high and 6.5 meters wide at the bottom, built in 1088, 3rd year of the Yuanyou reign of the Song Dynasty, by the astronomers Su Song, Han Gonglian and others in Bianjing (now Kaifeng, Henan Province). This model is based on the book *Exploitation of the Works of Nature*.

8-3-5 **Bronze human figure showing points for acupuncture and moxibustion** Cast in the Ming Dynasty, overall length 213 cm, with 666 acupoints. Modeled on a figure made in the Song Dynasty, this bronze figure was used not only in acupuncture therapy, but also in teaching and examinations at medical academies.

8-3-4

8-3-5*

8-3-5

8-3-6*

8-3-6

8-3-6 Bronze cannon inscribed with characters   Yuan Dynasty, full length 35.3 cm, weight 6.94 kilograms; unearthed in 1935 in Juyun Temple, Fangshan, Beijing. The body of the cannon bears an inscription that reads in translation, "3rd year of the Zhishun reign." It is the earliest bronze cannon with date discovered anywhere in the world.

8-3-7 Pottery cannon balls with caltrop design   Relics of the Yuan and Ming dynasties (13th-14th centuries).

8-3-7

8-3-8

8-3-8 Restored model of Bi Sheng's movable clay type   Northern Song. During the Qingli reign (1041-1048) of the Northern Song, Bi Sheng invented typography. He made small pieces of clay, carved an inverted character in relief on one end of each piece, then hardened the pieces by firing, forming in this way movable clay type for use in printing. The model shown here is based on the book *Notes Made at Dream Brook*.

8-3-9 Model of suspension-type compass   Northern Song, height 38 cm, length of each side of the base frame 21.5 cm. A magnetic needle is attached with wax to a piece of silk thread and hung in the center of the wooden frame, pointing north and south. This type of compass is very sensitive.

8-3-9

Yuan Dynasty (1271-1368), Period of Great Unity

From the 12th to the early 13th century, Mongol tribes inhabiting the Mongolian grassland grew steadily in strength. In 1206, the Mongol chieftain Temujin united various tribes on the grassland and established the Greater Mongolian State. He was given the honorable title Genghis Khan (Universal Ruler). Later, he and his successors continued their military expansion. At the height of its power, the Greater Mongolian State comprised northern China and parts of Central Asia and Europe. In 1260 Kublai Khan, Genghis Khan's grandson, succeeded to the throne and four years later moved his capital to Dadu (now Beijing). In 1271 he changed the name of his empire to Yuan, and in 1279 conquered the Southern Song. By this time the Yuan Dynasty was in control of all territory formerly under the Western Xia, Jin and Southern Song, unifying the whole of China, including present-day Xinjiang, Yunnan and Tibet.

During the reigns of the Mongol khans of Yuan, agriculture in the north recovered, cultivated land increased and irrigation works were expanded. The handicraft industry also made new progress, notably in the techniques of making porcelain and applying glaze. To facilitate transportation between the north and south, new river channels were built, the Grand Canal, constructed during the Sui and Tang dynasties, was rebuilt, and navigation routes on the sea were opened. Both domestic and foreign trade prospered, conducing to extensive economic and cultural exchanges between China and foreign countries. Science and culture of the Yuan Dynasty were pluralistic and intermixed in nature. Its achievements in astronomy and mathematics were in the forefront of the world. Yuan *qu*, a new form of literature, appeared while painting and calligraphy also reached new heights.

But national and class contradictions became increasingly acute, and this eventually led to the outbreak of a nationwide peasant uprising. In 1368 Zhu Yuanzhang established the Ming Dynasty at Nanjing. He advanced north, attacked and seized Dadu, and overthrew the Yuan Dynasty.

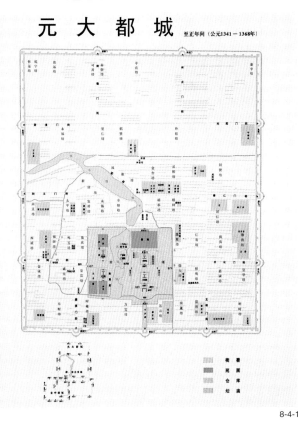

元 大 都 城 至正年间（公元1341－1368年）

8-4-1

8-4-2

8-4-1 Map of Dadu, capital of the Yuan Dynasty After succeeding to the throne, Kublai Khan built Dadu to the northeast of the Jin Dynasty's Middle Capital. This map was made on the basis of archaeological excavations.

8-4-2 Carved stone with twin-phoenix, twin-unicorn design Yuan structural element, 105 cm long, 120 cm wide, 13 cm thick; unearthed in 1966 from beneath a Ming Dynasty city wall in the western part of the Beijing Huapi Mill.

8-4-3*

8-4-4

8-4-5

8-4-3 Rafts on Lugou Yuan painting, 143.6 x 105 cm.

8-4-4 Pear-shaped vase with flared lip and pattern of interwining chrysanthemum in underglaze red Yuan Dynasty, height 32.1 cm, mouth diameter 8.4 cm, belly diameter 20.1 cm, base diameter 12.2 cm. Underglaze red was a creation of the Yuan Dynasty. The glaze contained copper and after firing assumed a red color that appeared to be within or under the glaze.

8-4-5 Celadon pear-shaped vase with flared lip and cloud-dragon design Yuan Dynasty, height 29.8 cm, mouth diameter 8.4 cm, base diameter 9.9 cm. The techniques of making celadon were already known during the Tang and Song dynasties, but were not widely used. It was not until the Yuan that celadon wares became popular.

8-4-6 Vase with interwining peony, product of Longquan Kiln Yuan Dynasty, height 45.5 cm, mouth diameter 19.5 cm, base diameter 13 cm; unearthed in 1970 from the ruins of Fengzhou City in the eastern suburbs of Huhhot, Inner Mongolia Autonomous Region. Longquan Kiln was located in present-day Longquan County, Zhejiang Province. It began operation in the Northern Song and continued to produce ceramics down to the Yuan. Its products belong to the category of celadons.

8-4-7 Vase with openwork stand, product of Jun Kiln Yuan Dynasty, height 58.3 cm, mouth diameter 17 cm, base diameter 18 cm; unearthed in 1970 from the ruins of Fengzhou City of the Yuan Dynasty, eastern suburbs of Huhhot, Inner Mongolia Autonomous Region. The Jun Kiln was located in what is now Yu County, Henan Province. Its products are in the category of northern celadons.

8-4-8 White-glazed porcelain jar with picture of a child traced in black, product of Cizhou Kiln Yuan Dynasty, height 30 cm, mouth diameter 18.5 cm, belly diameter 31 cm, base diameter 12 cm; discovered in 1994 near a sunken ship off the coast of Sandaogang, Suizhong County, Liaoning Province by the Underwater Archaeological Team of the National Museum of Chinese History.

8-4-6

8-4-7

8-4-8*

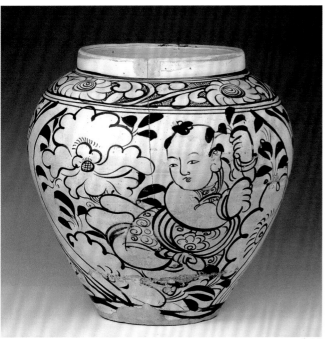

8-4-8

A member of the National Museum's Underwater Archaeological Team at work

8-4-9

8-4-9 Iron board with Arabic numerals Yuan Dynasty, 14.2 cm square; unearthed in 1965 from the ruins of the palace of the Prince of Anxi at Xi'an, Shaanxi Province. This is a magic square, in which the numbers in each row, column, and diagonal all add up to the same sum. It originated in Arabia and was introduced into China during the Yuan.

8-4-10 Porcelain bowl of Longquan Kiln Yuan

Dynasty, mouth diameter 17 cm; recovered in 1969 from a sunken ship found off the coast of Wenzhou Island, Zhuhai, Guangdong Province. Porcelain wares were among the principal exports of the Yuan. The bowl shown here was a part of a large cargo of porcelain carried by the ship.

8-4-11 Bronze tank water clock Device for measuring time made in 1316, the third year of the Yanyou reign of the Yuan Dynasty. It consisted of four tanks — sun tank, moon tank, star tank and water receiving tank. The sun tank was 75.5 cm tall, 68.2 cm in diameter at the top and 60 cm at the base; the moon tank 58.5 cm tall, 54.5 cm in diameter at the top and 53 cm at the base; the star tank 55.4 cm tall, 44 cm in diameter at the top and 39 cm at the base; and the water receiving tank 75 cm tall, 32 cm in diameter at the top and 31 cm at the base. This is the earliest multiple tank water clock discovered to date.

8-4-10

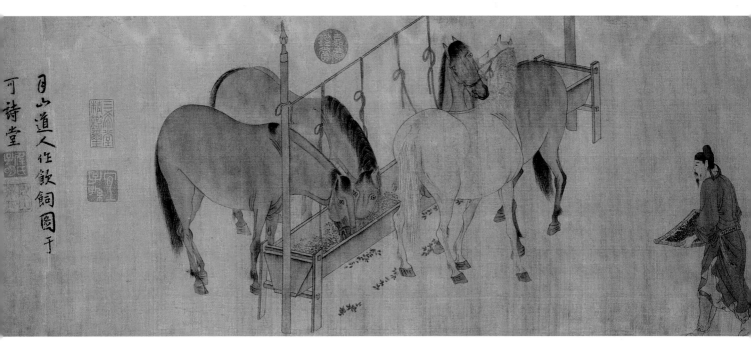

8-4-13

8-4-11

8-4-12 "Watering and Feeding" by Ren Renfa
Yuan painting, 29.7 x 186.5 cm. Ren Renfa
(1255-1327) was a native of Qinglong of
Songjiang Prefecture (now Shanghai). He
excelled in painting horses but was also good
at doing human figures and birds-and-flowers.
**8-4-13 Pottery figurines playing flute and
striking clappers** Yuan funerary objects,
height of figurines 38.5 cm and 36.5 cm
respectively; unearthed in 1965 from a Yuan
tomb in Xifeng Village, Jiaozuo, Henan
Province.

8-4-12

Ming Dynasty (1368—1644)

After more than twenty years of peasant wars during the last years of the Yuan Dynasty, Zhu Yuanzhang established the Ming Dynasty in Nanjing in 1368 and titled his reign Hongwu. In the same year, he captured the Yuan capital Dadu (now Beijing), overthrew the Yuan Dynasty, and unified the country. Zhu Yuanzhang adopted a series of measures that brought about a rapid recovery of the country's agriculture and handicraft industry. Politically, he strengthened the centralization of state power, holding all political and military power in his own hands. In 1421, the 19th year of the Yongle reign of Zhu Di, the third Ming emperor who was styled Chengzu, the capital was moved to Beijing. But most of the emperors of the mid- and late Ming were mediocre, and eunuchs and influential ministers arrogated all powers to themselves. Soon the government could no longer function properly and life became miserable for the masses. In 1644, a peasant uprising led by Li Zicheng toppled the dynasty.

Establishment of the Ming Dynasty

In 1368, Zhu Yuanzhang established the Ming Dynasty in Nanjing, proclaiming himself emperor. He conquered the Yuan Dynasty in the same year and gradually unified the country. He carried out reforms in both the central and local governments.

The Zhongshu Sheng (cabinet) and system of ministers were abolished. A *wei-suo* system of units was set up in the army's rank and file, and a five-army command established at the central level. All political and military power was in the hands of the emperor. The Ming government also strengthened its administration in the border regions, which helped promote the development of the unified, multi-national country.

9-1-1 Portrait of Zhu Yuanzhang Zhu Yuanzhang (1328-1398) was the first emperor of the Ming Dynasty.
9-1-2 "Palace City in Beijing" Painting of the mid-Ming Dynasty, 163 x 97 cm.

9-1-1

9-1-2

9-1-3

9-1-4

9-1-3 Empress Xiaojing's phoenix coronet Ming Dynasty, overall height 48.5 cm, coronet height 27 cm, diameter 23.7 cm, weight 2,320 grams; unearthed in 1957 from the Dingling Mausoleum in Beijing.

9-1-4 Xuande bronze bell and pestle Buddhist objects of the Ming Dynasty, overall height of bell 19.5 cm, mouth diameter 9.5 cm, length of pestle 12.7 cm. The two Buddhist objects were presented to the Potala Palace in Tibet by the Ming government during the Xuande reign (1426-35).

9-1-5 Scroll painting showing the successful quelling of a rebellion (section) Ming Dynasty, 43.8 x 971.2 cm. The painting depicts the whole process of how Ming troops put down a rebellion by ethnic minorities in the northwest in the early years of the Wanli reign (1573-1619).

9-1-5

Economy and Social Life

During the early Ming Dynasty, a series of measures were taken to revive and develop agriculture and the handicraft industry. Peasants were encouraged to farm and weave, and to reclaim wasteland. Emigrants and soldiers were organized to reclaim wasteland and build irrigation works; handicraftsmen were organized to serve by turns in the capital, though later such service could be exempted by payment of silver. As a result, peasants and craftsmen showed initiative and enthusiasm in their work, and both agriculture and handicrafts developed rapidly. The acreage of cultivated land was expanded, grain yield per unit area increased, planting of paddy-rice was greatly promoted, and cotton was introduced into the north to be planted on a large scale. Agricultural production reached a new high. Spinning and weaving, porcelain making, metallurgy and shipbuilding all made new progress, laying the foundation for the commercial prosperity of the country. In the mid and late Ming, the buds of a new capitalist mode of production appeared in the textile industry south of the Yangtze. Clothing, food, housing, transportation, festive recreation, religion and cultural life – all were rich and colorful in the Ming Dynasty.

9-2-1

9-2-2

9-2-3

9-2-1 "Tilling at Dawn" Painting of the Ming Dynasty, 172.6 x 107.9 cm. It depicts peasants working in the fields south of the Yangtze River.

9-2-2 Blue and white flask with cloud-dragon-seawater design Ming relic, Xuande reign (1426-1435), height 46.3 cm, mouth diameter 8 cm, base diameter 14.8 cm.

9-2-3 Five-color covered jar with fish-and-alga design Ming relic, Jiajing reign (1522-1566), overall height 35.3 cm, mouth diameter 17.7 cm, base diameter 24.8 cm.

9-2-4 Copper incense burner with cloud design Ming relic, Xuande reign (1426-1435), overall height 91.9 cm.

9-2-5 "The Splendor of an Imperial Capital" (section) Ming Dynasty, complete scroll 32 cm x 2,177.8 cm. It depicts busy scenes in Beijing, the imperial capital, during the mid-Ming.

9-2-4

9-2-5

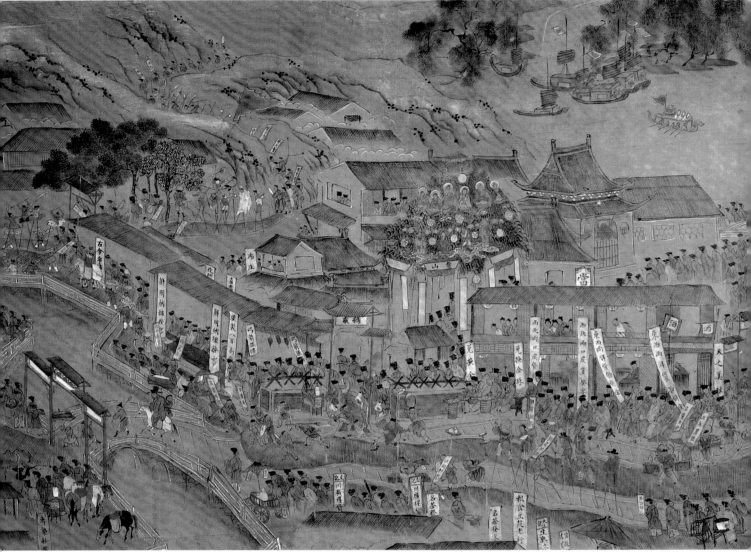

9-2-6

9-2-7

9-2-8*

9-2-6 "Thriving Southern Capital" (section)
Ming Dynasty, complete scroll 44 x 350 cm. It
shows the commercial prosperity of Nanjing,
the southern capital, during the mid-Ming.

**9-2-7 "Lantern Festival Celebrated in
Emperor Xianzong's Palace"** (section)
Painted in 1485, 21st year of the Chenghua
reign, Ming Dynasty, complete scroll 37 x 624
cm. Depicting scenes of fireworks, lantern
displays, and performances of magic and
acrobatics, it is a realistic portrayal of
celebrations in the Imperial Palace during the
Lantern Festival (15th day of the 1st month of
the Chinese lunar calendar).

**9-2-8 Cream-colored glazed porcelain statue
of Buddha Amitabba** Wanli reign (1573-
1619) of the Ming Dynasty, overall height
62.6 cm.

9-2-8

Culture, Science and Technology

With the development of mercantile economy and the appearance of the seeds of capitalism, trends of enlightened thought reflecting reality emerged in the fields of philosophy, science and literature. In philosophy, a thinker named Li Zhi appeared, who opposed traditional feudal dogmatism and hypocritical Taoism. *Book Burning* and *Book Holding* are two of his major works which have been preserved to the present. In the scientific field were such prominent men like Li Shizhen, Xu Xiake, Xu Guangqi and Song Yingxing, authors of *Compendium of Materia Medica, Travels of Xu Xiake, Exploitation of the Works of Nature* and *A Complete Treatise on Agriculture* respectively. In literature, there appeared a type of novel called *zhanghui* with each chapter headed by a couplet giving the gist of its contents. Representative works are Luo Guanzhong's *Romance of the Three Kingdoms,* Shi Nai'an's *Outlaws of the Marsh* and Wu Cheng'en's *Journey to the West.* Painting and the arts and crafts also made new progress. Wen Zhengming, Shen Zhou and Tang Yin, famous painters of the mid-Ming, founded the school of literati painting. In the arts and crafts, the quintessence was the technique of filigreeing on enamel (also known as cloisonné). One of the greatest Chinese encyclopedic works of all time, the *Yongle Encyclopedia,* was compiled during the Ming. It was completed in five years by 3,000 scholars headed by Xie Jin and organized by the Ming government.

9-3-1

9-3-1 Portrait of Xu Xiake Xu Xiake (1586-1641), original name Hongzu, a native of Jiangyin in present-day Jiangsu Province, was a renowned traveler and geographer of the Ming Dynasty. *Travels of Xu Xiake* is his most famous work.

9-3-2

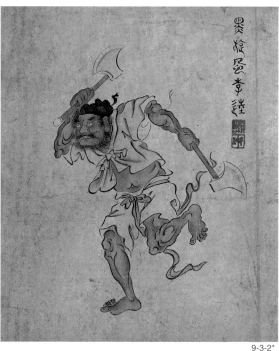

9-3-2*

9-3-3

9-3-4

9-3-4 **Cloisonné bowl with fish and seaweed design and high stem** Ming Dynasty, height 10.4 cm, mouth diameter 14.9 cm, stem diameter 4 cm.
9-3-5 **"Reclining Rock and Old Plum"** Painting by Chen Hongshou, Ming Dynasty, 74.5 x 43.5 cm.
9-3-6 *Compendium of Materia Medica* Compiled by Li Shizhen (1518-1593), a masterpiece of pharmacology of the Ming Dynasty.

9-3-2 **Section of scroll painting on figures in** *Outlaws of the Marsh* The original painting was done by Chen Hongshou (1597- 1652), styled Laolian. This is an imitation made by a Qing Dynasty artist. *Outlaws of the Marsh* is a novel based on peasant uprisings led by Song Jiang. It was written by Shi Nai'an of the late Ming and early Qing.
9-3-3 **Prince Lu's** *zhong he* **lute** Stringed instrument of the Ming Dynasty, overall length 120 cm. Carved on the back of the lute are two characters *zhong he*, which may be translated as "the golden mean and harmony," an ideal state in Chinese classical aesthetics.

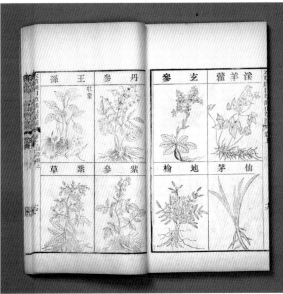

9-3-6

9-3-5

Foreign Relations

The Ming Dynasty developed friendly ties with many of its neighboring countries. Between the Yongle reign and Xuande reign (c.1405-1433), the Ming government sent Zheng He, with a large fleet, to the "Western Oceans" on seven occasions. These voyages greatly promoted China's friendly relations with many Asian and African countries. During the Jiajing reign, Japanese pirates ravaged China's southeastern coasts, causing great suffering to the Chinese people. Qi Jiguang, a general, and other patriots drove away the marauders. At the end of the 16th century, Chinese soldiers and civilians helped the Korean army drive out Japanese invaders from the Korean peninsula.

9-4-2

9-4-1 Zheng He's big bronze bell Ming Dynasty, overall height 83 cm, mouth diameter 49 cm. The bell was cast in Fujian in 1431, the 6th year of the Xuande reign, during Zheng He's seventh voyage to the "Western Oceans."

9-4-2 "Presenting a Unicorn from Bengal" Original painting by Shen Du of the Ming Dynasty, 118.3 x 46.5 cm. The one shown here was copied by Qing artist Chen Zhang.

9-4-1*

9-4-1

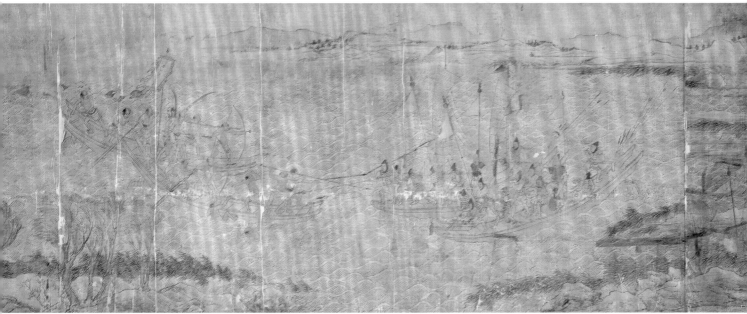

9-4-3 Large Japanese bronze mirror
Diameter 76.5 cm, weight 46.25 kilograms;
unearthed in Quanzhou, Fujian Province. This
mirror was made in Japan during the Edo
period, and brought to China in the late Ming.
9-4-4 "Fighting the Japanese Pirates" (section)
Scroll painting of the Ming Dynasty, 31.1 x
572.7 cm.

9-4-3

9-4-4

Decline of the Ming Dynasty

During the mid- and late Ming Dynasty, bureaucrats, aristocrats, royal kinsmen and other wealthy people plundered and annexed the land of the peasantry on a massive scale. The number of landless peasants soared, their burdens made heavier by the excessive taxes levied by the government. Most of the Ming emperors of this period were incompetent and dissolute, and all power at court was in the hands of eunuchs and despotic ministers. Zhang Juzheng, a capable politician, introduced a number of political and economic reforms that proved to be successful during the early years of the Wanli reign, but the success was short-lived. The reforms were annulled after his death. Meanwhile, the Nuzhen tribe in the northeast built up its strength and established the Later Jin regime, which became a serious threat to the Ming court. Natural calamities also occurred frequently during the last years of the Ming, further aggravating the lot of the common people. Finally, in 1627, Wang Er, a peasant in Shaanxi Province, launched a large-scale peasant uprising and, in 1644, a peasant army led by Li Zicheng occupied Beijing and overthrew the Ming Dynasty.

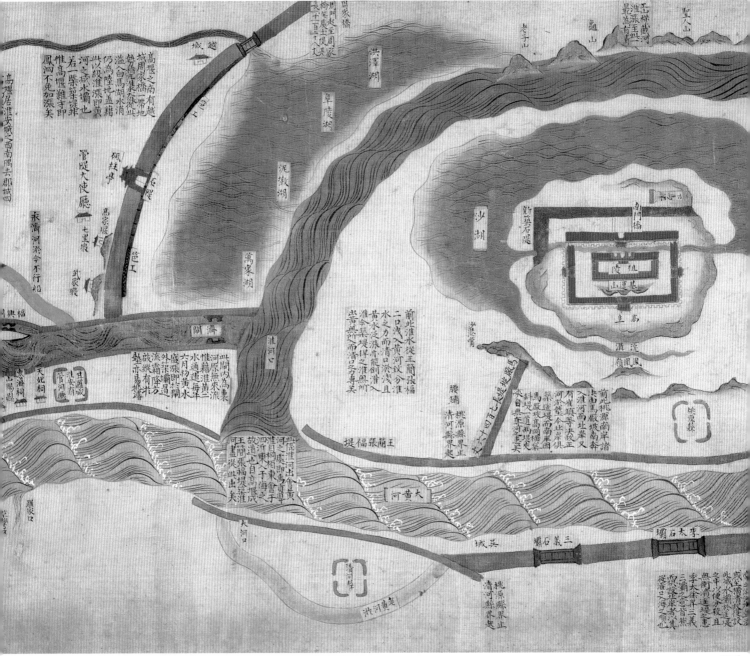

9-5-2

9-5-4

9-5-1 "A Survey of Flood Prevention Works" (section)
Painted by Pan Jixun in 1590, 18th year of the Wanli
reign, Ming Dynasty, complete scroll 45 x 1,959 cm. The
painting reflects Pan Jixun's lifelong dedication to the
harnessing of the Yellow River and Grand Canal.

9-5-2 Wooden seal of imperial guards   Ming relic, 14th
year (1478) of the Chenghua reign, 4 cm high, each side
of seal-face 11.5 cm long.

9-5-3 Wei Dazhong's last written words
Ming Dynasty. Wei Dazhong (1575-1629), a member of
the Donglin Dang, a political clique of scholar-officials,
was persecuted to death by the Yan Dang, a clique
faithful to the powerful eunuch Wei Zhongxian of the
late Ming.

**9-5-4 Copper seal of "Garrison Reclamation
Department under the Governmental Public Works"**
Seal of the Dashun regime set up by Li Zicheng, 1st year
(1644) of the Yongchang reign, height 10.2 cm, length of
each side 8.5 cm; unearthed in 1959 at Wangfujing,
Beijing.

9-5-4*

9-5-3

Qing Dynasty   (1644—1911)

The Qing Dynasty was the last feudal dynasty in China. After capturing Beijing, its leaders set up a system of control over the whole country. Most of its governmental policies followed those of the Ming Dynasty, except that the Manchu nobility was now in a dominant position. Decisions on important military and administrative affairs were made by the Conference of Princes Regent, the highest policy-making organ, whose powers surpassed those of the cabinet and six ministries. During the reigns of Kangxi and Qianlong, the Qing government annihilated the separatist forces of Wu Sangui and others, strengthening its control over the border regions and stabilizing the country's frontiers. The country enjoyed a period of social stability, solid national strength and progress in science and culture. On its vast territory, the solidarity of different nationalities was continually strengthened, and Han and ethnic minorities fought shoulder to shoulder against foreign invaders to safeguard their unity. But after the reign of Emperor Qianlong, internal and external contradictions intensified, and struggles against Qing rule increased. In 1840, the 20th year of the Daoguang reign, the Opium War, an armed invasion of China by foreign capitalism, broke out. The Qing government was forced to sign a series of unequal treaties, which gradually reduced China to the status of a semi-colonial, semi-feudal country. Bitter anti-imperialist, anti-feudal struggles followed, but it was not until the Revolution of 1911, in the third year of the Xuantong reign, that the Chinese people overthrew the Qing imperial dynasty which had ruled China for 268 years.

Establishment of the Qing Dynasty

In the late 16th century, the Nuzhen tribe in northeastern China grew steadily in strength under the leadership of its chieftain Nurhachi, who established the Later Jin regime. During the reign of his son, Huangtaiji, the name Jin was changed to Qing. In 1644, with the connivance of Wu Sangui, a Ming general guarding Shanhai Pass, Qing troops entered this strategic pass and defeated a peasant army led by Li Zicheng. Following this victory, the Qing regime moved its capital from Shenyang to Beijing to begin its 268-year rule over China. The Han people south of the pass stubbornly resisted the Qing army and it was only after more than 20 years of war that the Qing Dynasty finally unified the whole of China, including Taiwan. In the early years of the dynasty, Manchu aristocrats dominated the government, but after Emperor Kangxi set up his Southern Study and Emperor Yongzheng set up the Ministry of Defense, intellectuals of the Han nationality were allowed to participate in state affairs.

10-1-1 Huangtaiji's order plate for moving troops Tiancong and Chongde reigns (1627-1643) of the Qing Dynasty, length 20.3 cm, width 31.2 cm.
10-1-2 Picture of Duoduo entering Nanjing Qing Dynasty, 142.1 x 112 cm. Duoduo was the 15th son of Nurhachi.
10-1-3 Portrait of Zheng Chenggong Qing Dynasty, 130.5 x 65 cm. Zheng Chenggong (1624-1662) was a national hero. In 1661 he led a fleet to Taiwan, drove out the Dutch colonialists, and recovered the island.

10-1-1

10-1-2

10-1-3

10-1-4 Jade seal "Treasure of Emperor"
Qing Dynasty, overall height 16.1 cm, each
side of seal face 10.1 cm, height of knob
9.8 cm.

10-1-4

10-1-4*

10-1-5

10-1-5 Portrait of Emperor Kangxi Qing
Dynasty, 98.2 x 68.1 cm. Kangxi (1654-1722)
was a capable emperor of the early Qing who
reigned a total of 61 years. His given name
was Aisin-Gioro Xuanye, and his temple
name Shengzu. Kangxi was the title of his
reign.

**10-1-6 Armor and helmet of Emperor
Qianlong** Qing Dynasty, length of armor
130 cm, height of helmet 63 cm.

10-1-6*

10-1-6

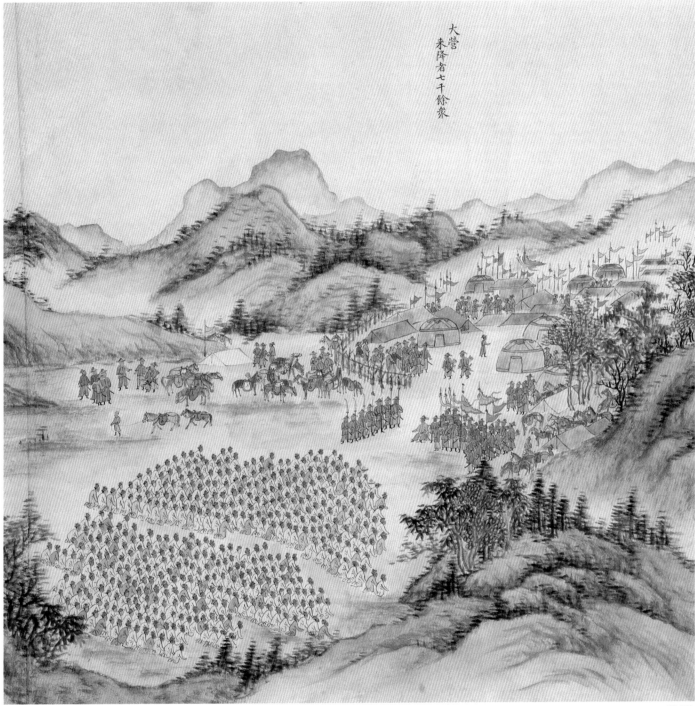

大營
來降者七千餘眾

10-1-7

10-1-7 Scroll painting "Suppressing the Junggar Rebellion" (section) Qing Dynasty, complete scroll 41 x 808 cm. This section depicts 7,000 rebels surrendering.

10-1-8 Gold seal presented by the Qing government to the Dalai Lama Qing Dynasty, height 9.9 cm, each side of seal-face 11.3 cm.

10-1-8

10-1-8*

Economy and Social Life

Agriculture saw great progress in the Qing Dynasty. Notable achievements were made in harnessing the Yellow and Huai rivers; grain yield per unit area increased; and planting of cash crop was widely promoted. Textiles, porcelain making, mining, iron-smelting all made rapid progress. The development of agriculture and handicrafts helped promote the growth of mercantile economy. Thriving cities emerged in great numbers, and new commercial cities such as Urumqi appeared in remote border areas.

Social life of the various nationalities was rich and colorful. Food, clothing, housing, marriages and funerals, seasonal festivals, cultural entertainments, transportation, communications, customs and habits, welfare and relief, all developed in their own ways. Exchanges of knowledge and information among the nationalities facilitated social development and improved living standards.

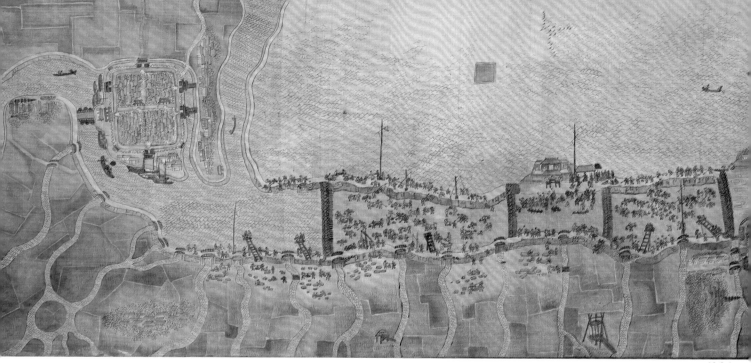

10-2-1

10-2-2

10-2-3*

10-2-3

10-2-1 "Projects Undertaken to Harness the Huai River" (section) Painted by Zhao Cheng in the 8th year of the Shunzhi reign, Qing Dynasty. Complete scroll 46.3 x 543.5 cm.

10-2-2 "Transportation on the Lu River" (section) Scroll painting of the Qing Dynasty, 41.5 x 675 cm. It depicts a bustling scene at the Tongzhou section of the north- south Grand Canal.

10-2-3 Celestial-body vase with sea-water and posy design in contending colors Yongzheng reign (1723-1735) of the Qing Dynasty, height 52.2 cm, mouth diameter 11.5 cm, base diameter 16.5 cm.

10-2-4

10-2-4 Sky-clearing blue glazed *haiyan heqing* jar Qianlong reign (1736-1795) of the Qing Dynasty, height 31.3 cm, mouth diameter 25.1 cm, base diameter 22.7 cm.

10-2-4*

10-2-5*

10-2-5 "Busy Street Scenes at Qianmen, Beijing" Section of scroll painting "Emperor Qianlong's Inspection Tours to South China", Qing Dynasty, 72.6 x 2178 cm.

10-2-5

10-2-6

10-2-6 **"Special Envoys"** (section) Scroll
painting by Jin Tingbiao of the Qing Dynasty,
33.8 x 1438 cm.

10-2-7 **"Wedding Day"** (section) Painting of
the Qing Dynasty, 35 x 369.5 cm.

10-2-8 **Famille-rose Duomu pot** Qianlong
reign (1736-1795) of the Qing Dynasty, height
45 cm, mouth diameter 13.6 cm, product of
the Guan Kiln. The pot was used to drink
milk by Mongolians and Tibetans living in
the palace.

10-2-7

10-2-8

10-2-9*

10-2-9

10-2-9 Tibetan bronze ewer with dragon-shaped handle Qing Dynasty, height 33.8 cm, mouth diameter 8.5 cm.
10-2-10 Famille-rose openwork vase with a movable core Qing Dynasty, height 30.3 cm, mouth diameter 8.5 cm, base diameter 10.5 cm.

10-2-10

Culture, Science and Technology

Quite a few thinkers with rudimentary democratic ideology and materialist trends of thought emerged in the early Qing Dynasty, the most famous being Gu Yanwu, Huang Zongxi and Wang Fuzhi. Social and economic progress and the introduction of Western scientific and technological knowledge also helped promote the development of the natural sciences in China, notably astronomy, calendrical systems and mathematics, in which outstanding achievements were made. *New Methods of Xiao'en* by astronomer Wang Xichan improved upon certain methods of calculation in astronomy, and mathematician Ming Antu was the first to study π by analytic methods. Famous works by outstanding novelists and dramatists such as *Strange Tales from Liaozhai*, *The Scholars*, *A Dream of Red Mansions* and *Peach-Blossom Fan* are still being avidly read today. In the fine arts, diverse schools of painting appeared and with it a large number of celebrated painters. The handicraft industry turned out numerous superb and colorful works. Voluminous encyclopedic works such as the *Encyclopedia of Ancient and Modern Books*, *Complete Library in Four Divisions* and *Twenty-Four Dynastic Histories* were compiled under the auspices of the government.

10-3-1

10-3-1 Portrait of Gu Yanwu Gu Yanwu (1613-1682), styled Ningren, also known as Tinglin, was a native of Kunshan (in today's Jiangsu Province). He was a famous thinker and scholar of the late Ming and early Qing who put forward the famous slogan, "Every individual is responsible for the rise and fall of his country."

10-3-2 Celestial globe made by Qi Yanhuai Qing Dynasty, overall height 34 cm, distance between legs 24.5 cm. Qi Yanhuai (1774-1841) was a native of Wuyuan (in present-day Jiangxi Province) and a scientist who made outstanding contributions to the study of astronomy and farm irrigation.

10-3-2

10-3-3*

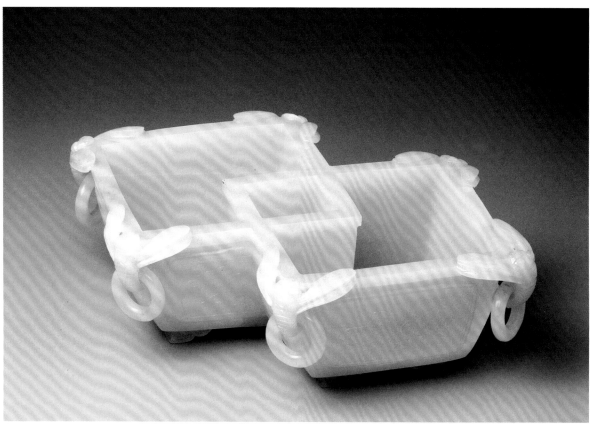

10-3-3 Album on *Strange Tales from Liaozhai* Qing Dynasty, 45.7 x 34.9 cm (half page). The paintings are based on Pu Songling's (1640-1715) collection *Strange Tales from Liaozhai*.

10-3-4 Jade twin-washer decorated with six dragonflies and rings Qing Dynasty, height 6.3 cm, length 23.3 cm, width 15.4 cm.

10-3-3

10-3-4

秋草秋花照碧游雪
鋤顧影鬟珍綠別開
生面原恆語可矢曾
閒日再思
己卯素御題

臣鄒一桂恭畫

10-3-5 "Hibiscus and Twin Egrets"
Painting by Zou Yigui of the Qing Dynasty,
113 x 94 cm. Zou Yigui (1686-1772), a native
of Wuxi (in today's Jiangsu Province), was a
celebrated painter of the Qing Dynasty.

**10-3-6 Red lacquer alms bowl with copper
core and seven-Buddha design** Qing
Dynasty, height 10.5 cm, mouth diameter
11.6 cm.

10-3-6*

10-3-5

10-3-6

Economic and Cultural Exchanges with Foreign Countries in the Early Qing

After the Qing government united Taiwan with the rest of the country, restrictions on overseas trade were lifted and trade ports opened. Chinese silk, tea and porcelain were exported in large quantities through these ports. Government envoys were dispatched on mutual visits between China and other countries, and friendly intercourse among the common people were also frequent. Korean writing paper and folding fans became popular with the Chinese people; Japanese lacquerware and *qibaoshao* ("firing seven treasures"), a traditional Japanese enamel craft, enjoyed a high repute in China; and elephant tusks from Vietnam, bronzeware and jadeware from India were imported in quantity. European commodities, too, made their way into China in an endless stream and in their wake came Western science and technology.

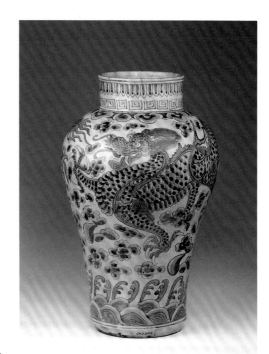

10-4-1

10-4-1 Korean blue and white vase with cloud-and-dragon design　Imported in early Qing, height 51.6 cm, mouth diameter 17.5 cm, base diameter 18 cm.

10-4-2 Big Japanese pen holder with landscape design traced in gold on black lacquer ground　Imported in early Qing, height 22.8 cm, diameter 21.2 cm.

10-4-2

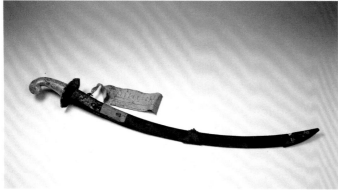

10-4-3

10-4-3 Elephant tusks from Vietnam
Imported in early Qing, length 150 cm, diameter of upper end 12 cm.

10-4-4 British saber with jasper inlaid handle and leather sheath　Gift to Qing Emperor Qianlong from George Macartney, a British envoy; overall length 97.7 cm. In 1793, the 58th year of Qianlong's reign, the British government sent G. Macartney as an envoy to demand that China relax its restrictions on trade. The demand was rejected by the Qing government.

10-4-4

10-4-4*

Decline of the Qing Dynasty

During the late Qing, government officials became extremely corrupt and the people lived in dire poverty. Natural and man-made calamities befell one after another, and peasant uprisings occurred from time to time. This eventually led to the rebellion known as the Taiping Heavenly Kingdom Uprising that swept most parts of the country, greatly shaking the rule of the Qing court. Beginning in the 1840's, the Western powers had launched in succession the Opium War, the Second Opium War, the Sino-French War, the Sino-Japanese War and the Eight-Power Allied Forces invasion, forcing China to sign a series of unequal treaties, which seriously encroached upon China's sovereignty and territory. After the Sino-Japanese War, imperialist powers began to lease land in China, set up banks and export capital to China. By way of economic aggression, they exerted an ever greater influence over the Chinese government. China sank deeper and deeper into the abyss of semi-colonialism while the Qing government became increasingly corrupt and incompetent.

Table of Major Unequal Treaties Signed in the Late Qing

Name of Treaty	Date	Main Terms
Sino-British Treaty of Nanjing	August 29,1842	1.China opens Guangzhou, Fuzhou, Xiamen, Ningbo and Shanghai as trade ports. 2.China cedes Hong Kong to Britain. 3.China pays Britain an indemnity of 21 million silver dollars. 4.Tariff on British goods are subject to negotiations between China and Britain.
Sino-British Treaty of Tianjin	June 26, 1858	1.China opens Niuzhuang, Dengzhou, Tainan, Chaozhao, Qiongzhou, Hankou, Jiujiang, Nanjing, Zhenjiang as trade ports. 2.British warships are allowed to sail into the trade ports. 3.Christian and Catholic missionaries are free to carry out missionary activities in China's interior. 4.China pays Britain an indemnity of 4 million taels of silver.
Sino-French Treaty of Tianjin	June 27, 1858	1.China opens Qiongzhou, Chaozhou, Tainan, Danshui, Dengzhou and Nanjing as trade ports. 2.French warships are allowed to sail into the trade ports. 3.Christian and Catholic missionaries are free to carry out missionary activities in China's interior. 4.China pays France an indemnity of 2 million taels of silver.
Sino-British Convention of Beijing	October 24,1860	1.China opens Tianjin as a trade port. 2.China cedes a part of Kowloon to Britain. 3.China pays Britain an indemnity of 8 million taels of silver.
Sino-French Convention of Beijing	October 25,1860	1.China opens Tianjin as a trade port. 2.China pays France an indemnity of 8 million taels of silver.
Sino-Japanese Treaty of Shimonoseki	April 17, 1895	1.China cedes to Japan Liaodong Peninsula, Penghu Islands, Taiwan and its adjacent islands. 2.China pays Japan an indemnity of 200 million taels of silver. 3.China opens Shashi, Chongqing, Suzhou and Hangzhou as trade ports; Japanese vessels are allowed to sail into these ports along China's inland rivers. 4.Japan is allowed to open factories in China's trade ports. 5.Japanese goods manufactured in China are exempt from taxation; Japan is allowed to set up warehouses in China's interior.
Treaty of 1901	September 7, 1901	1.China is to pay eleven countries (Britain, U.S., Russia, Germany, Austria, France, Italy, Japan, Belgium, Spain and Holland) an indemnity of 450 million taels of silver within 39 years. The unpaid balance carries an annual interest of 4 per cent. 2.Foreign countries are allowed to station troops in Beijing, and along the railway line between Beijing and Shanghai Pass; the fort at Dagu and all forts from Dagu to Beijing are dismantled. 3.A legation quarter is set up in Beijing's Dongjiaominxiang where foreign countries are allowed to station troops. 4.The Qing government is to inflict severe punishment on "chief offenders, including ministers," and forbids the Chinese people to set up or participate in anti-imperialist organizations; violaters are to be put to death.

10-5-1 Opium smoking set Late Qing; height of lamp 10 cm, diameter 7.6 cm; height of opium holder 4.8 cm, diameter 6.5 cm; height of opium case 3.4 cm, diameter 3.8 cm; length of pipe 60 cm. Beginning in the mid-18th century, Britain had been exporting opium to China, poisoning the Chinese people physically and spiritually. This is an opium smoking set used at that time.

10-5-1

10-5-2

10-5-3

10-5-4

10-5-5

10-5-2 Hong Kong Oil painting of Late Qing, 57.5 x 89 cm. After the signing of the Nanjing Treaty in 1842, China ceded Hong Kong to Britain. The painting depicts Hong Kong in its early days as a treaty port.

10-5-3 Macao Oil painting of Late Qing, 49 x 62.5 cm. After the Opium War, Portugal further encroached upon China's sovereign rights in Macao. The painting shows Macao during the late Qing.

10-5-4 Brass knocker on the door of Taojia Study, Yuanmingyuan Garden Late Qing. During the Second Opium War, the British-French allied forces burnt down the Yuanmingyuan Garden (Garden of Perfect Splendor). This brass knocker was on the door of a study in Hualinlong Hall, Changchun Yard, in the Yuanmingyuan Garden.

10-5-5 Extant volume from the *Complete Library in Four Divisions* Late Qing. The volume was stored in the Wenyuan Pavilion, Yuanmingyuan Garden.

10-5-6 Land certificate of the Taiping Heavenly Kingdom Late Qing, length 26 cm, width 22 cm. It

10-5-6

10-5-7

was issued when a new land system was adopted by the Taiping Heavenly Kingdom.

10-5-7 Heavenly Kingdom coins Late Qing. The coins were issued by the Taiping Heavenly Kingdom.

10-5-8 Banknotes issued in China by foreign banks Circulated in the late Qing. In the last years of the Qing Dynasty, some imperialist countries set up banks in China and issued banknotes so as to export capital to China.

10-5-8

Economy and Culture of the Late Qing

During the late years of the Qing Dynasty, the social economy and culture of China underwent unprecedented changes. Since the mid-19th century, certain feudal bureaucrats, in the name of acquiring wealth and power for China, had been using the country's financial resources to purchase foreign machines and other equipment, employ foreign technicians and set up new-type industries. Some landlord merchants also operated and invested in modern industries. The Qing government, too, embarked on such newly emerging enterprises as building railways and ships, installing telegraph and telephone systems, setting up banks, post offices, etc. Modern universities, museums, libraries and publishing houses began to appear. In literature, novels that censured and satirized the collusion of local officials with foreigners became the fashion. World-famous works translated by Lin Shu and others enabled the people to see and hear new things. Books on modern science and technology such as mathematics, physics, chemistry, acoustics and electricity were very popular.

10-6-2

10-6-3

10-6-1 Textile carding machine Imported from Britain in 1895 during the late Qing; weight 4 tons. It was used in the Dasheng Cotton Mill founded by Zhang Jian.

10-6-2 Large Dragon Stamps Late Qing. They are China's earliest stamps.

10-6-3 Telephone set Late Qing; height 25 cm, length of side of base 20 cm. China's earliest telephone set.

10-6-4 Paper currency issued by the Great Qing Bank in the late Qing.

10-6-4

10-6-1

10-6-5 Scroll painting of flowers and birds
By Ren Bonian; 120 x 55 cm. Ren Yi (1840-1896), styled Bonian, was a famous painter of the late Qing.

10-6-6 Manuscript of *The Travels of Lao Can*
By Liu E (1857-1909) of the late Qing.

10-6-6

End of the Last Imperial Dynasty and
Establishment of a Republic

Imperialist aggression had intensified during the late Qing and the Qing government, increasingly corrupt, was weak and helpless. Bourgeois democratic thinking gradually developed in the country, and bourgeois revolutionaries headed by Sun Yat-sen appeared. The founding of the Chinese Revolutionary League in 1905 marked the beginning of a bourgeois revolutionary party in China. The revolutionaries carried out a series of bitter and heroic armed struggles against the Qing government. On October 10, 1911, an uprising in Wuchang, Hubei Province, succeeded and the next day a military government was established in the province. Other provinces in the south quickly followed suit, declaring their independence from the Qing. On January 1, 1912, the Provisional Government of the Republic of China was founded, with Sun Yat-sen as provisional president, and on February 12, 1912, the last Qing emperor Puyi announced his abdication, ending the feudal monarchic system that had ruled China for more than two thousand years.

10-7-3

10-7-1

10-7-2

10-7-1 *Soul of the Yellow Emperor, Book of Grievances and* The Zhejiang Tide   Publications of the late Qing, published by bourgeois thinkers to promote anti-Manchu revolution.

10-7-2 Grave of 72 Martyrs of Huanghuagang   On April 27, 1911, the Chinese Revolutionary League launched an anti-Qing armed uprising in Guangzhou. It was defeated, and later the bodies of 72 martyrs were found and buried together at Huanghuagang in the suburbs of Guangzhou. They are known in history as the 72 Martyrs of Huanghuagang.

10-7-3 18-star flag (replica)   Late Qing; length 280 cm, width 165 cm. After the success of the Wuchang Uprising, the Hubei Military Government used this flag for a time. It was one of the national flags of the Republic of China.

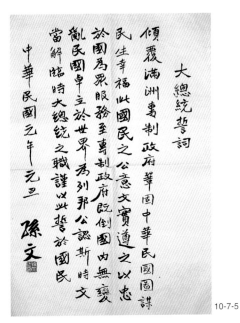

10-7-5

10-7-4 Statue of Sun Yat-sen Sun Yat-sen (1866-1925) was a leader of the Chinese bourgeois revolution. He was also called Sun Wen. At one time he used an assumed name, Zhongshan Qiao.

10-7-5 Oath made by the Provisional President (copy) The oath was made on January 1, 1912, when Sun Yat-sen took office.

10-7-4

10-7-6 Imperial edict on the abdication of the Qing emperor (copy) This imperial edict announcing the abdication of the Qing emperor Puyi was made on February 12, 1912.

10-7-7 Extra issue of *Capital Bulletin* It carries the imperial edict on the abdication of the Qing emperor.

10-7-6

10-7-7

Chronological Table of the Exhibition of Chinese History

Palaeolithic Age	c. 1.7 million — 10,000 Y.B.P.
Neolithic Age	c. 10,000 — 4,000 Y.B.P.
Xia	c. 21st — 16th century BC
Shang	c. 16th — 11th century BC
Western Zhou	c. 11th century — 771 BC
Spring & Autumn	770 — 476 BC
Warring States	475 — 221 BC
Qin	221 — 206 BC
Western Han	206 BC — AD 8
Eastern Han	25 — 220
Three Kingdoms	220 — 265
Western Jin	265 — 316
Eastern Jin	317 — 420
Northern Dynasties	386 — 581
Southern Dynasties	420 — 589
Sui	581 — 618
Tang	618 — 907
Five Dynasties	907 — 960
Liao	916 — 1125
Northern Song	960 — 1127
Southern Song	1127 — 1279
Western Xia	1038 — 1227
Jin	1115 — 1234
Yuan	1271 — 1368
Ming	1368 — 1644
Qing	1644 — 1911

One of the Halls of the Exhibition of Chinese History

National Museum of Chinese History

Postscript

The four-volume serial publication *A Journey into China's Antiquity* (published by the Morning Glory Publishers) was compiled by the National Museum of Chinese History to represent graphically the Exhibition of Chinese History on permanent display in the museum. It is in the category of high-grade, de luxe art books of which only limited editions are printed. In consideration of the diverse needs and interests of our readers, we have now compiled this medium-grade, one-volume illustrated catalogue of the exhibits. It bears the same title as the exhibition and is designed to present as rich a collection of photos as possible in a much more limited space, with clear and concise explanations and in an attractive and elegant format. To this end, we have put together a choice collection of the most important photos in *A Journey into China's Antiquity*, augmented with a fairly large number of photos of relics and exhibits not included in the four volumes, thus providing a more comprehensive though less detailed view of the Exhibition of Chinese History. Chinese, English and Japanese language editions of the catalogue have been published simultaneously.

The compilation and writing of the text of the catalogue was organized by the Exhibition Department of the museum. The text writers for the different sections were: An Jiayuan and Sun Qigang, Paleolithic and Neolithic ages; Dong Qi, Xia, Shang, Western Zhou and Spring and Autumn period; Wang Guanying, Warring States period; Chen Chengjun and Wang Yonghong, Qin, Western Han and Eastern Han; Shao Wenliang and Shao Xiaomeng, Three Kingdoms period, two Jin dynasties and Northern and Southern Dynasties; Kong Xiangxing and Hu Xiaojian, Sui, Tang and Five Dynasties; Zheng Enhuai, Huang Yansheng and Chen Yu, Liao, Song, Western Xia, Jin and Yuan; Liu Ruzhong, Li Zefeng and Wang Fang, Ming and Qing; Li Xuemei and Su Shengwen, late Qing. Li Ji did the planning and collation of the manuscripts and wrote the Preface and Postscript. Yu Weichao and Du Yaoxi were in overall charge of the compilation and examining of manuscripts. Photographs of archaeological sites, underwater archaeological work and aerial surveys were provided by the Archaeological Department of the museum.

The Editors

Beijing 1998

图书在版编目(CIP)数据

中国通史陈列: 英文 / 中国历史博物馆编.
北京: 朝华出版社, 1998.1
ISBN 7-5054-0559-4

Ⅰ. 中…
Ⅱ. 中…
Ⅲ. 文物－中国－画册
Ⅳ. K87-64

中国版本图书馆CIP数据核字(98)第02090号

中国通史陈列

(英文版)

中国历史博物馆编

中国 北京 天安门广场东侧　邮政编码 100006

朝华出版社出版

中国 北京 车公庄西路 35 号　邮政编码 100044

北京恒信邦和彩色印刷有限公司

中国 北京 朝阳区龙王堂工业区　邮政编码 100012

中国国际图书贸易总公司发行

中国 北京 车公庄西路 35 号
北京邮政信箱 399 号　邮政编码 100044

新华书店经销

1998 年第 1 版 2002 年第 2 次印刷
ISBN 7-5054-0559-4/J.0282
09750
85-E-515P

中华人民共和国印制